卞尺丹几乙し丹卞と
Translated Language Learning

The Communist Manifesto

Manifesto Komunis

Karl Marx & Friedrich Engels

English / Bahasa Melayu

Copyright © 2024 Tranzlaty

All rights reserved.

Published by Tranzlaty

ISBN: 978-1-83566-468-1

Original text by Karl Marx and Friedrich Engels

The Communist Manifesto

First published in 1848

www.tranzlaty.com

Introduction
Pengenalan

A spectre is haunting Europe — the spectre of Communism
Hantu menghantui Eropah - hantu Komunisme
All the Powers of old Europe have entered into a holy alliance to exorcise this spectre
Semua Kuasa Eropah lama telah memasuki pakatan suci untuk mengusir hantu ini
Pope and Czar, Metternich and Guizot, French Radicals and German police-spies
Paus dan Tsar, Metternich dan Guizot, Radikal Perancis dan pengintip polis Jerman
Where is the party in opposition that has not been decried as Communistic by its opponents in power?
Di manakah parti pembangkang yang tidak dikecam sebagai Komunis oleh lawannya yang berkuasa?
Where is the Opposition that has not hurled back the branding reproach of Communism, against the more advanced opposition parties?
Di manakah pembangkang yang tidak melemparkan kembali celaan penjenamaan Komunisme, terhadap parti pembangkang yang lebih maju?
And where is the party that has not made the accusation against its reactionary adversaries?
Dan di manakah parti yang tidak membuat tuduhan terhadap musuh-musuhnya yang reaksioner?
Two things result from this fact
Dua perkara terhasil daripada fakta ini
I. Communism is already acknowledged by all European Powers to be itself a Power
I. Komunisme sudah diakui oleh semua Kuasa Eropah sebagai Kuasa itu sendiri
II. It is high time that Communists should openly, in the face of the whole world, publish their views, aims and tendencies

II. Sudah tiba masanya Komunis harus secara terbuka, di hadapan seluruh dunia, menerbitkan pandangan, matlamat dan kecenderungan mereka

they must meet this nursery tale of the Spectre of Communism with a Manifesto of the party itself

mereka mesti memenuhi kisah kanak-kanak Hantu Komunisme ini dengan Manifesto parti itu sendiri

To this end, Communists of various nationalities have assembled in London and sketched the following Manifesto

Untuk tujuan ini, Komunis dari pelbagai bangsa telah berkumpul di London dan melakar Manifesto berikut

this manifesto is to be published in the English, French, German, Italian, Flemish and Danish languages

manifesto ini akan diterbitkan dalam bahasa Inggeris, Perancis, Jerman, Itali, Flemish dan Denmark

And now it is to be published in all the languages that Tranzlaty offers

Dan kini ia akan diterbitkan dalam semua bahasa yang ditawarkan oleh Tranzlaty

Bourgeois and the Proletarians
Borjuis dan Proletar

The history of all hitherto existing societies is the history of class struggles
Sejarah semua masyarakat yang sedia ada sehingga kini adalah sejarah perjuangan kelas
Freeman and slave, patrician and plebeian, lord and serf, guild-master and journeyman
Orang bebas dan hamba, bangsawan dan plebeian, tuan dan hamba, ketua persatuan dan pengembara
in a word, oppressor and oppressed
dalam satu perkataan, penindas dan tertindas
these social classes stood in constant opposition to one another
kelas-kelas sosial ini sentiasa bertentangan antara satu sama lain
they carried on an uninterrupted fight. Now hidden, now open
mereka meneruskan perjuangan tanpa gangguan. Kini tersembunyi, kini dibuka
a fight that either ended in a revolutionary re-constitution of society at large
perjuangan yang sama ada berakhir dengan perlembagaan semula masyarakat yang revolusioner secara amnya
or a fight that ended in the common ruin of the contending classes
atau pergaduhan yang berakhir dengan kehancuran bersama kelas-kelas yang bersaing
let us look back to the earlier epochs of history
Mari kita lihat kembali kepada zaman sejarah yang terdahulu
we find almost everywhere a complicated arrangement of society into various orders
kita dapati hampir di mana-mana susunan masyarakat yang rumit ke dalam pelbagai susunan
there has always been a manifold gradation of social rank

sentiasa ada penggredan kedudukan sosial yang bermacam-macam

In ancient Rome we have patricians, knights, plebeians, slaves

Di Rom purba kita mempunyai bangsawan, kesatria, plebeian, hamba

in the Middle Ages: feudal lords, vassals, guild-masters, journeymen, apprentices, serfs

pada Zaman Pertengahan: tuan-tuan feudal, pengikut, tuan persatuan, pengembara, perantis, hamba

in almost all of these classes, again, subordinate gradations

Dalam hampir semua kelas ini, sekali lagi, penggredan bawahan

The modern Bourgeoisie society has sprouted from the ruins of feudal society

Masyarakat Borjuasi moden telah tumbuh dari runtuhan masyarakat feudal

but this new social order has not done away with class antagonisms

Tetapi tatanan sosial baru ini tidak menghapuskan antagonisme kelas

It has but established new classes and new conditions of oppression

Ia telah menubuhkan kelas baru dan keadaan penindasan baru

it has established new forms of struggle in place of the old ones

ia telah menubuhkan bentuk-bentuk perjuangan baru menggantikan yang lama

however, the epoch we find ourselves in possesses one distinctive feature

Walau bagaimanapun, zaman yang kita dapati mempunyai satu ciri tersendiri

the epoch of the Bourgeoisie has simplified the class antagonisms

zaman Borjuasi telah memudahkan antagonisme kelas

Society as a whole is more and more splitting up into two great hostile camps

Masyarakat secara keseluruhan semakin berpecah kepada dua kem bermusuhan yang besar

two great social classes directly facing each other: Bourgeoisie and Proletariat

dua kelas sosial yang hebat berhadapan secara langsung antara satu sama lain: Borjuasi dan Proletariat

From the serfs of the Middle Ages sprang the chartered burghers of the earliest towns

Dari hamba Zaman Pertengahan muncul penduduk bertauliah bandar-bandar terawal

From these burgesses the first elements of the Bourgeoisie were developed

Daripada burgesses ini unsur-unsur pertama Borjuasi telah dibangunkan

The discovery of America and the rounding of the Cape

Penemuan Amerika dan pembulatan Cape

these events opened up fresh ground for the rising Bourgeoisie

peristiwa-peristiwa ini membuka landasan baru untuk Borjuasi yang semakin meningkat

The East-Indian and Chinese markets, the colonisation of America, trade with the colonies

Pasaran Hindia Timur dan Cina, penjajahan Amerika, berdagang dengan tanah jajahan

the increase in the means of exchange and in commodities generally

peningkatan dalam cara pertukaran dan komoditi secara amnya

these events gave to commerce, navigation, and industry an impulse never before known

Peristiwa-peristiwa ini memberi kepada perdagangan, navigasi, dan industri dorongan yang tidak pernah diketahui sebelum ini

it gave rapid development to the revolutionary element in the tottering feudal society

ia memberi perkembangan pesat kepada unsur revolusioner dalam masyarakat feudal yang terhuyung-huyung

closed guilds had monopolised the feudal system of industrial production

Persatuan tertutup telah memonopoli sistem feudal pengeluaran perindustrian

but this no longer sufficed for the growing wants of the new markets

Tetapi ini tidak lagi mencukupi untuk keperluan pasaran baharu yang semakin meningkat

The manufacturing system took the place of the feudal system of industry

Sistem pembuatan menggantikan sistem industri feudal

The guild-masters were pushed on one side by the manufacturing middle class

Tuan persatuan ditolak di satu pihak oleh kelas pertengahan pembuatan

division of labour between the different corporate guilds vanished

Pembahagian kerja antara persatuan korporat yang berbeza lenyap

the division of labour penetrated each single workshop

Pembahagian kerja menembusi setiap bengkel tunggal

Meantime, the markets kept ever growing, and the demand ever rising

Sementara itu, pasaran terus berkembang, dan permintaan semakin meningkat

Even factories no longer sufficed to meet the demands

Malah kilang-kilang tidak lagi mencukupi untuk memenuhi permintaan

Thereupon, steam and machinery revolutionised industrial production

Selepas itu, wap dan jentera merevolusikan pengeluaran perindustrian

The place of manufacture was taken by the giant, Modern Industry

Tempat pembuatan diambil oleh gergasi, Industri Moden

the place of the industrial middle class was taken by industrial millionaires

Tempat kelas menengah perindustrian diambil oleh jutawan industri

the place of leaders of whole industrial armies were taken by the modern Bourgeoisie

tempat pemimpin seluruh tentera perindustrian telah diambil oleh Borjuasi moden

the discovery of America paved the way for modern industry to establish the world market

penemuan Amerika membuka jalan kepada industri moden untuk menubuhkan pasaran dunia

This market gave an immense development to commerce, navigation, and communication by land

Pasaran ini memberikan perkembangan yang besar kepada perdagangan, navigasi, dan komunikasi melalui darat

This development has, in its time, reacted on the extension of industry

Perkembangan ini, pada masanya, telah bertindak balas terhadap peluasan industri

it reacted in proportion to how industry extended, and how commerce, navigation and railways extended

ia bertindak balas mengikut perkadaran bagaimana industri diperluaskan, dan bagaimana perdagangan, navigasi dan kereta api diperluaskan

in the same proportion that the Bourgeoisie developed, they increased their capital

dalam bahagian yang sama yang dibangunkan oleh Borjuasi, mereka meningkatkan modal mereka

and the Bourgeoisie pushed into the background every class handed down from the Middle Ages

dan Borjuasi menolak ke latar belakang setiap kelas yang diturunkan dari Zaman Pertengahan

therefore the modern Bourgeoisie is itself the product of a long course of development
oleh itu Borjuasi moden itu sendiri adalah hasil daripada perjalanan pembangunan yang panjang

we see it is a series of revolutions in the modes of production and of exchange
kita melihat ia adalah satu siri revolusi dalam mod pengeluaran dan pertukaran

Each developmental Bourgeoisie step was accompanied by a corresponding political advance
Setiap langkah Borjuasi pembangunan disertai dengan kemajuan politik yang sepadan

An oppressed class under the sway of the feudal nobility
Kelas yang tertindas di bawah pengaruh bangsawan feudal

an armed and self-governing association in the mediaeval commune
sebuah persatuan bersenjata dan pemerintahan sendiri di komune zaman pertengahan

here, an independent urban republic (as in Italy and Germany)
di sini, sebuah republik bandar yang merdeka (seperti di Itali dan Jerman)

there, a taxable "third estate" of the monarchy (as in France)
di sana, "estet ketiga" monarki yang boleh dikenakan cukai (seperti di Perancis)

afterwards, in the period of manufacture proper
selepas itu, dalam tempoh pembuatan yang betul

the Bourgeoisie served either the semi-feudal or the absolute monarchy
Borjuasi berkhidmat sama ada monarki separa feudal atau mutlak

or the Bourgeoisie acted as a counterpoise against the nobility
atau Borjuasi bertindak sebagai penentang terhadap golongan bangsawan

and, in fact, the Bourgeoisie was a corner-stone of the great monarchies in general

dan, sebenarnya, Borjuasi adalah batu penjuru monarki besar secara amnya

but Modern Industry and the world-market established itself since then

tetapi Industri Moden dan pasaran dunia menubuhkan dirinya sejak itu

and the Bourgeoisie has conquered for itself exclusive political sway

dan Borjuasi telah menakluki untuk dirinya sendiri pengaruh politik eksklusif

it achieved this political sway through the modern representative State

ia mencapai pengaruh politik ini melalui Negara perwakilan moden

The executives of the modern State are but a management committee

Eksekutif Negara moden hanyalah sebuah jawatankuasa pengurusan

and they manage the common affairs of the whole of the Bourgeoisie

dan mereka menguruskan hal ehwal bersama seluruh Borjuasi

The Bourgeoisie, historically, has played a most revolutionary part

Borjuasi, dari segi sejarah, telah memainkan peranan yang paling revolusioner

wherever it got the upper hand, it put an end to all feudal, patriarchal, and idyllic relations

di mana sahaja ia mendapat kelebihan, ia menamatkan semua hubungan feudal, patriarki, dan indah

It has pitilessly torn asunder the motley feudal ties that bound man to his "natural superiors"

Ia telah merobek tanpa belas kasihan hubungan feudal beraneka ragam yang mengikat manusia dengan "atasan semula jadi"

and it has left remaining no nexus between man and man, other than naked self-interest

dan ia telah meninggalkan tiada hubungan antara manusia dan manusia, selain daripada kepentingan diri yang telanjang

man's relations with one another have become nothing more than callous "cash payment"

hubungan manusia antara satu sama lain telah menjadi tidak lebih daripada "pembayaran tunai" yang tidak berperasaan

It has drowned the most heavenly ecstasies of religious fervour

Ia telah menenggelamkan kegembiraan keagamaan yang paling syurga

it has drowned chivalrous enthusiasm and philistine sentimentalism

ia telah menenggelamkan semangat kesatria dan sentimentalisme filistin

it has drowned these things in the icy water of egotistical calculation

ia telah menenggelamkan perkara-perkara ini dalam air berais pengiraan egois

It has resolved personal worth into exchangeable value

Ia telah menyelesaikan nilai peribadi kepada nilai yang boleh ditukar

it has replaced the numberless and indefeasible chartered freedoms

ia telah menggantikan kebebasan bertauliah yang tidak terkira dan tidak dapat dinafikan

and it has set up a single, unconscionable freedom; Free Trade

dan ia telah menubuhkan kebebasan tunggal yang tidak masuk akal; Perdagangan Bebas

In one word, it has done this for exploitation

Dalam satu perkataan, ia telah melakukan ini untuk eksploitasi

exploitation veiled by religious and political illusions

eksploitasi yang diselubungi oleh ilusi agama dan politik

exploitation veiled by naked, shameless, direct, brutal
exploitation

eksploitasi terselubung oleh eksploitasi telanjang, tidak tahu
malu, langsung, kejam

the Bourgeoisie has stripped the halo off every previously
honoured and revered occupation

Borjuasi telah menanggalkan lingkaran cahaya dari setiap
pekerjaan yang dihormati dan dihormati sebelum ini

the physician, the lawyer, the priest, the poet, and the man
of science

doktor, peguam, imam, penyair, dan ahli sains

it has converted these distinguished workers into its paid
wage labourers

ia telah menukar pekerja terkemuka ini kepada buruh upah
bergaji

The Bourgeoisie has torn the sentimental veil away from the
family

Borjuasi telah merobek tudung sentimental daripada keluarga

and it has reduced the family relation to a mere money
relation

dan ia telah mengurangkan hubungan keluarga kepada
hubungan wang semata-mata

the brutal display of vigour in the Middle Ages which
Reactionists so much admire

paparan kekuatan yang kejam pada Zaman Pertengahan yang
sangat dikagumi oleh Reaksionis

even this found its fitting complement in the most slothful
indolence

walaupun ini mendapati pelengkapnya yang sesuai dalam
kemalasan yang paling malas

The Bourgeoisie has disclosed how all this came to pass

Borjuasi telah mendedahkan bagaimana semua ini berlaku

The Bourgeoisie have been the first to show what man's
activity can bring about

Borjuasi telah menjadi yang pertama menunjukkan apa yang
boleh dibawa oleh aktiviti manusia

It has accomplished wonders far surpassing Egyptian pyramids, Roman aqueducts, and Gothic cathedrals

Ia telah mencapai keajaiban yang jauh melebihi piramid Mesir, saluran air Rom, dan katedral Gothic

and it has conducted expeditions that put in the shade all former Exoduses of nations and crusades

dan ia telah menjalankan ekspedisi yang meletakkan di bawah naungan semua bekas Keluaran bangsa-bangsa dan perang salib

The Bourgeoisie cannot exist without constantly revolutionising the instruments of production

Borjuasi tidak boleh wujud tanpa sentiasa merevolusikan instrumen pengeluaran

and thereby it cannot exist without its relations to production

dan dengan itu ia tidak boleh wujud tanpa hubungannya dengan pengeluaran

and therefore it cannot exist without its relations to society

dan oleh itu ia tidak boleh wujud tanpa hubungannya dengan masyarakat

all earlier industrial classes had one condition in common

Semua kelas perindustrian terdahulu mempunyai satu syarat yang sama

they relied on the conservation of the old modes of production

mereka bergantung pada pemuliharaan mod pengeluaran lama

but the Bourgeoisie brought with it a completely new dynamic

tetapi Borjuasi membawa bersamanya dinamik yang sama sekali baru

Constant revolutionizing of production and uninterrupted disturbance of all social conditions

Revolusi berterusan pengeluaran dan gangguan tanpa gangguan semua keadaan sosial

this everlasting uncertainty and agitation distinguishes the Bourgeoisie epoch from all earlier ones

ketidakpastian dan pergolakan yang kekal ini membezakan zaman Borjuasi daripada semua zaman terdahulu

previous relations with production came with ancient and venerable prejudices and opinions

hubungan terdahulu dengan pengeluaran datang dengan prasangka dan pendapat kuno dan dihormati

but all of these fixed, fast-frozen relations are swept away

tetapi semua hubungan yang tetap dan cepat beku ini dihanyutkan

all new-formed relations become antiquated before they can ossify

semua hubungan yang baru terbentuk menjadi lapuk sebelum ia boleh mengeras

All that is solid melts into air, and all that is holy is profaned

Semua yang pepejal cair ke udara, dan semua yang suci dicemari

man is at last compelled to face with sober senses, his real conditions of life

Manusia akhirnya terpaksa menghadapi dengan deria yang sedar, keadaan sebenar kehidupannya

and he is compelled to face his relations with his kind

dan dia terpaksa menghadapi hubungannya dengan jenisnya

The Bourgeoisie constantly needs to expand its markets for its products

Borjuasi sentiasa perlu mengembangkan pasarannya untuk produknya

and, because of this, the Bourgeoisie is chased over the whole surface of the globe

dan, kerana ini, Borjuasi dikejar di seluruh permukaan dunia

The Bourgeoisie must nestle everywhere, settle everywhere, establish connections everywhere

Borjuasi mesti bersarang di mana-mana, menetap di mana-mana, mewujudkan hubungan di mana-mana

The Bourgeoisie must create markets in every corner of the world to exploit

Borjuasi mesti mewujudkan pasaran di setiap pelosok dunia untuk mengeksploitasi

the production and consumption in every country has been given a cosmopolitan character

pengeluaran dan penggunaan di setiap negara telah diberi watak kosmopolitan

the chagrin of Reactionists is palpable, but it has carried on regardless

kekecewaan Reaksionis dapat dirasai, tetapi ia telah berterusan tanpa mengira

The Bourgeoisie have drawn from under the feet of industry the national ground on which it stood

Borjuasi telah menarik dari bawah kaki industri tanah negara di mana ia berdiri

all old-established national industries have been destroyed, or are daily being destroyed

semua industri negara yang lama ditubuhkan telah musnah, atau setiap hari dimusnahkan

all old-established national industries are dislodged by new industries

Semua industri negara yang lama ditubuhkan disingkirkan oleh industri baru

their introduction becomes a life and death question for all civilised nations

pengenalan mereka menjadi persoalan hidup dan mati bagi semua negara bertamadun

they are dislodged by industries that no longer work up indigenous raw material

mereka disingkirkan oleh industri yang tidak lagi menggunakan bahan mentah asli

instead, these industries pull raw materials from the remotest zones

sebaliknya, industri ini menarik bahan mentah dari zon terpencil

industries whose products are consumed, not only at home, but in every quarter of the globe
industri yang produknya digunakan, bukan sahaja di rumah, tetapi di setiap suku dunia
In place of the old wants, satisfied by the productions of the country, we find new wants
Sebagai ganti kehendak lama, berpuas hati dengan pengeluaran negara, kita dapati kehendak baru
these new wants require for their satisfaction the products of distant lands and climes
kehendak baru ini memerlukan untuk kepuasan mereka produk tanah dan iklim yang jauh
In place of the old local and national seclusion and self-sufficiency, we have trade
Sebagai ganti pengasingan dan sara diri tempatan dan kebangsaan yang lama, kami mempunyai perdagangan
international exchange in every direction; universal inter-dependence of nations
pertukaran antarabangsa dalam setiap arah; Kebergantungan sejagat negara
and just as we have dependency on materials, so we are dependent on intellectual production
dan sama seperti kita mempunyai kebergantungan kepada bahan, begitu juga kita bergantung kepada pengeluaran intelektual
The intellectual creations of individual nations become common property
Ciptaan intelektual setiap negara menjadi harta bersama
National one-sidedness and narrow-mindedness become more and more impossible
Keberat sebelah dan fikiran sempit negara menjadi semakin mustahil
and from the numerous national and local literatures, there arises a world literature
dan daripada banyak kesusasteraan kebangsaan dan tempatan, timbul kesusasteraan dunia

by the rapid improvement of all instruments of production

dengan peningkatan pesat semua instrumen pengeluaran

by the immensely facilitated means of communication

dengan cara komunikasi yang sangat dipermudahkan

The Bourgeoisie draws all (even the most barbarian nations) into civilisation

Borjuasi menarik semua (walaupun negara yang paling biadab) ke dalam tamadun

The cheap prices of its commodities; the heavy artillery that batters down all Chinese walls

Harga murah komoditinya; artileri berat yang menghantam semua tembok China

the barbarians' intensely obstinate hatred of foreigners is forced to capitulate

kebencian orang barbar yang sangat degil terhadap orang asing terpaksa menyerah kalah

It compels all nations, on pain of extinction, to adopt the Bourgeoisie mode of production

Ia memaksa semua negara, atas kesakitan kepupusan, untuk mengamalkan cara pengeluaran Borjuasi

it compels them to introduce what it calls civilisation into their midst

ia memaksa mereka untuk memperkenalkan apa yang dipanggil tamadun ke tengah-tengah mereka

The Bourgeoisie force the barbarians to become Bourgeoisie themselves

Borjuasi memaksa orang barbar untuk menjadi Borjuasi sendiri

in a word, the Bourgeoisie creates a world after its own image

dalam satu perkataan, Borjuasi mencipta dunia mengikut imejnya sendiri

The Bourgeoisie has subjected the countryside to the rule of the towns

Borjuasi telah menundukkan kawasan luar bandar kepada pemerintahan bandar-bandar

It has created enormous cities and greatly increased the urban population

Ia telah mewujudkan bandar-bandar besar dan meningkatkan penduduk bandar dengan ketara

it rescued a considerable part of the population from the idiocy of rural life

ia menyelamatkan sebahagian besar penduduk daripada kebodohan kehidupan luar bandar

but it has made those in the the countryside dependent on the towns

tetapi ia telah menjadikan mereka yang berada di luar bandar bergantung kepada bandar-bandar

and likewise, it has made the barbarian countries dependent on the civilised ones

dan begitu juga, ia telah menjadikan negara-negara biadab bergantung kepada negara-negara bertamadun

nations of peasants on nations of Bourgeoisie, the East on the West

bangsa-bangsa petani di negara-negara Borjuasi, Timur di Barat

The Bourgeoisie does away with the scattered state of the population more and more

Borjuasi menghapuskan keadaan penduduk yang bertaburan semakin banyak

It has agglomerated production, and has concentrated property in a few hands

Ia mempunyai pengeluaran yang terkumpul, dan mempunyai harta tertumpu di beberapa tangan

The necessary consequence of this was political centralisation

Akibat yang diperlukan daripada ini ialah pemusatan politik

there had been independent nations and loosely connected provinces

Terdapat negara merdeka dan wilayah yang bersambung longgar

they had separate interests, laws, governments and systems
of taxation

mereka mempunyai kepentingan, undang-undang, kerajaan
dan sistem percukaian yang berasingan

but they have become lumped together into one nation, with
one government

tetapi mereka telah disatukan menjadi satu negara, dengan
satu kerajaan

they now have one national class-interest, one frontier and
one customs-tariff

mereka kini mempunyai satu kepentingan kelas nasional, satu
sempadan dan satu tarif kastam

and this national class-interest is unified under one code of
law

dan kepentingan kelas nasional ini disatukan di bawah satu
kod undang-undang

the Bourgeoisie has achieved much during its rule of scarce
one hundred years

Borjuasi telah mencapai banyak perkara semasa
pemerintahannya yang terhad seratus tahun

more massive and colossal productive forces than have all
preceding generations together

kuasa produktif yang lebih besar dan besar daripada semua
generasi sebelumnya bersama-sama

Nature's forces are subjugated to the will of man and his
machinery

Kuasa alam semula jadi ditaklukkan kepada kehendak
manusia dan jenteranya

chemistry is applied to all forms of industry and types of
agriculture

Kimia digunakan untuk semua bentuk industri dan jenis
pertanian

steam-navigation, railways, electric telegraphs, and the
printing press

navigasi wap, kereta api, telegraf elektrik, dan mesin cetak

clearing of whole continents for cultivation, canalisation of rivers

pembersihan seluruh benua untuk penanaman, terusan sungai

whole populations have been conjured out of the ground and put to work

seluruh populasi telah disulap keluar dari tanah dan digunakan untuk bekerja

what earlier century had even a presentiment of what could be unleashed?

Apakah abad awal yang mempunyai prasentimen tentang apa yang boleh dilepaskan?

who predicted that such productive forces slumbered in the lap of social labour?

Siapa yang meramalkan bahawa kuasa produktif sedemikian tertidur di pangkuan buruh sosial?

we see then that the means of production and of exchange were generated in feudal society

kita melihat bahawa alat pengeluaran dan pertukaran telah dijana dalam masyarakat feudal

the means of production on whose foundation the Bourgeoisie built itself up

alat-alat pengeluaran di mana asasnya Borjuasi membina dirinya sendiri

At a certain stage in the development of these means of production and of exchange

Pada peringkat tertentu dalam pembangunan alat pengeluaran dan pertukaran ini

the conditions under which feudal society produced and exchanged

keadaan di mana masyarakat feudal menghasilkan dan bertukar

the feudal organisation of agriculture and manufacturing industry

Pertubuhan Feudal Pertanian dan Industri Pembuatan

the feudal relations of property were no longer compatible with the material conditions

hubungan feudal harta tidak lagi serasi dengan keadaan material

They had to be burst asunder, so they were burst asunder

Mereka terpaksa pecah, jadi mereka pecah

Into their place stepped free competition from the productive forces

Ke tempat mereka melangkah persaingan bebas daripada kuasa produktif

and they were accompanied by a social and political constitution adapted to it

dan mereka disertai dengan perlembagaan sosial dan politik yang disesuaikan dengannya

and it was accompanied by the economical and political sway of the Bourgeoisie class

dan ia disertai dengan pengaruh ekonomi dan politik kelas Borjuasi

A similar movement is going on before our own eyes

Pergerakan serupa sedang berlaku di hadapan mata kita sendiri

Modern Bourgeoisie society with its relations of production, and of exchange, and of property

Masyarakat Borjuasi moden dengan hubungan pengeluaran, dan pertukaran, dan harta benda

a society that has conjured up such gigantic means of production and of exchange

masyarakat yang telah memunculkan cara pengeluaran dan pertukaran yang begitu besar

it is like the sorcerer who called up the powers of the nether world

Ia seperti ahli sihir yang memanggil kuasa dunia bawah

but he is no longer able to control what he has brought into the world

tetapi dia tidak lagi dapat mengawal apa yang telah dia bawa ke dunia

For many a decade past history was tied together by a common thread

Selama sedekad yang lalu, sejarah telah diikat bersama oleh benang yang sama

the history of industry and commerce has been but the history of revolts

Sejarah industri dan perdagangan hanyalah sejarah pemberontakan

the revolts of modern productive forces against modern conditions of production

pemberontakan kuasa produktif moden terhadap keadaan pengeluaran moden

the revolts of modern productive forces against property relations

pemberontakan kuasa produktif moden terhadap hubungan harta

these property relations are the conditions for the existence of the Bourgeoisie

hubungan harta ini adalah syarat untuk kewujudan Borjuasi

and the existence of the Bourgeoisie determines the rules for property relations

dan kewujudan Borjuasi menentukan peraturan untuk hubungan harta

it is enough to mention the periodical return of commercial crises

Cukuplah untuk menyebut pengembalian krisis komersial secara berkala

each commercial crisis is more threatening to Bourgeoisie society than the last

setiap krisis komersial lebih mengancam masyarakat Borjuasi daripada yang terakhir

In these crises a great part of the existing products are destroyed

Dalam krisis ini, sebahagian besar produk sedia ada dimusnahkan

but these crises also destroy the previously created productive forces

Tetapi krisis ini juga memusnahkan kuasa produktif yang dicipta sebelum ini

in all earlier epochs these epidemics would have seemed an absurdity

Dalam semua zaman terdahulu, wabak ini kelihatan tidak masuk akal

because these epidemics are the commercial crises of over-production

kerana wabak ini adalah krisis komersial pengeluaran berlebihan

Society suddenly finds itself put back into a state of momentary barbarism

Masyarakat tiba-tiba mendapati dirinya kembali ke dalam keadaan kebiadaban seketika

as if a universal war of devastation had cut off every means of subsistence

seolah-olah perang kemusnahan sejagat telah memotong setiap cara sara hidup

industry and commerce seem to have been destroyed; and why?

industri dan perdagangan nampaknya telah musnah; Dan mengapa?

Because there is too much civilisation and means of subsistence

Kerana terdapat terlalu banyak tamadun dan cara sara hidup

and because there is too much industry, and too much commerce

dan kerana terdapat terlalu banyak industri, dan terlalu banyak perdagangan

The productive forces at the disposal of society no longer develop Bourgeoisie property

Kuasa produktif di pelupusan masyarakat tidak lagi membangunkan harta Borjuasi

on the contrary, they have become too powerful for these conditions, by which they are fettered

sebaliknya, mereka telah menjadi terlalu kuat untuk keadaan ini, yang mana mereka dibelenggu

as soon as they overcome these fetters, they bring disorder into the whole of Bourgeoisie society

sebaik sahaja mereka mengatasi belenggu ini, mereka membawa kekacauan ke dalam seluruh masyarakat Borjuasi

and the productive forces endanger the existence of Bourgeoisie property

dan kuasa produktif membahayakan kewujudan harta Borjuasi

The conditions of Bourgeoisie society are too narrow to comprise the wealth created by them

Keadaan masyarakat Borjuasi terlalu sempit untuk terdiri daripada kekayaan yang dicipta oleh mereka

And how does the Bourgeoisie get over these crises?

Dan bagaimana Borjuasi mengatasi krisis ini?

On the one hand, it overcomes these crises by the enforced destruction of a mass of productive forces

Di satu pihak, ia mengatasi krisis ini dengan pemusnahan paksa jisim kuasa produktif

on the other hand, it overcomes these crises by the conquest of new markets

Sebaliknya, ia mengatasi krisis ini dengan penaklukan pasaran baharu

and it overcomes these crises by the more thorough exploitation of the old forces of production

dan ia mengatasi krisis ini dengan eksploitasi yang lebih menyeluruh terhadap kuasa pengeluaran lama

That is to say, by paving the way for more extensive and more destructive crises

Maksudnya, dengan membuka jalan kepada krisis yang lebih meluas dan lebih merosakkan

it overcomes the crisis by diminishing the means whereby crises are prevented

ia mengatasi krisis dengan mengurangkan cara di mana krisis dicegah

The weapons with which the Bourgeoisie felled feudalism to the ground are now turned against itself

Senjata-senjata yang digunakan oleh Borjuasi menumbangkan feudalisme ke tanah kini berpaling menentang dirinya sendiri

But not only has the Bourgeoisie forged the weapons that bring death to itself

Tetapi bukan sahaja Borjuasi telah memalsukan senjata yang membawa kematian kepada dirinya sendiri

it has also called into existence the men who are to wield those weapons

ia juga telah memanggil kewujudan lelaki yang akan menggunakan senjata itu

and these men are the modern working class; they are the proletarians

dan orang-orang ini adalah kelas pekerja moden; mereka adalah proletar

In proportion as the Bourgeoisie is developed, in the same proportion is the Proletariat developed

Dalam perkadaran seperti Borjuasi dibangunkan, dalam perkadaran yang sama Proletariat dibangunkan

the modern working class developed a class of labourers

Kelas pekerja moden membangunkan kelas buruh

this class of labourers live only so long as they find work

Kelas buruh ini hidup hanya selagi mereka mendapat pekerjaan

and they find work only so long as their labour increases capital

dan mereka mencari kerja hanya selagi buruh mereka meningkatkan modal

These labourers, who must sell themselves piece-meal, are a commodity

Buruh-buruh ini, yang mesti menjual diri mereka sedikit demi sedikit, adalah komoditi

these labourers are like every other article of commerce

Buruh-buruh ini seperti setiap artikel perdagangan yang lain

and they are consequently exposed to all the vicissitudes of competition
dan akibatnya mereka terdedah kepada semua perubahan persaingan
they have to weather all the fluctuations of the market
Mereka perlu mengharungi semua turun naik pasaran
Owing to the extensive use of machinery and to division of labour
Disebabkan oleh penggunaan jentera yang meluas dan pembahagian kerja
the work of the proletarians has lost all individual character
kerja proletariat telah kehilangan semua watak individu
and consequently, the work of the proletarians has lost all charm for the workman
dan akibatnya, kerja proletar telah kehilangan semua daya tarikan bagi pekerja
He becomes an appendage of the machine, rather than the man he once was
Dia menjadi pelengkap mesin, dan bukannya lelaki seperti dulu
only the most simple, monotonous, and most easily acquired knack is required of him
Hanya bakat yang paling mudah, membosankan, dan paling mudah diperoleh diperlukan daripadanya
Hence, the cost of production of a workman is restricted
Oleh itu, kos pengeluaran seorang pekerja adalah terhad
it is restricted almost entirely to the means of subsistence that he requires for his maintenance
ia terhad hampir sepenuhnya kepada cara sara hidup yang dia perlukan untuk nafkahnya
and it is restricted to the means of subsistence that he requires for the propagation of his race
dan ia terhad kepada cara sara hidup yang dia perlukan untuk penyebaran kaumnya
But the price of a commodity, and therefore also of labour, is equal to its cost of production

Tetapi harga komoditi, dan oleh itu juga buruh, adalah sama dengan kos pengeluarannya

In proportion, therefore, as the repulsiveness of the work increases, the wage decreases

Oleh itu, dalam perkadaran, apabila kejijikan kerja meningkat, gaji berkurangan

Nay, the repulsiveness of his work increases at an even greater rate

Tidak, kejijikan karyanya meningkat pada kadar yang lebih tinggi

as the use of machinery and division of labour increases, so does the burden of toil

apabila penggunaan jentera dan pembahagian kerja meningkat, begitu juga beban kerja keras

the burden of toil is increased by prolongation of the working hours

Beban kerja keras ditingkatkan dengan memanjangkan waktu bekerja

more is expected of the labourer in the same time as before

lebih banyak diharapkan daripada buruh dalam masa yang sama seperti sebelum ini

and of course the burden of the toil is increased by the speed of the machinery

dan sudah tentu beban kerja keras ditingkatkan dengan kelajuan jentera

Modern industry has converted the little workshop of the patriarchal master into the great factory of the industrial capitalist

Industri moden telah menukar bengkel kecil tuan patriarki menjadi kilang besar kapitalis perindustrian

Masses of labourers, crowded into the factory, are organised like soldiers

Massa buruh, bersesak ke dalam kilang, diatur seperti askar

As privates of the industrial army they are placed under the command of a perfect hierarchy of officers and sergeants

Sebagai persendirian tentera perindustrian, mereka diletakkan di bawah perintah hierarki pegawai dan sarjan yang sempurna

they are not only the slaves of the Bourgeoisie class and State

mereka bukan sahaja hamba kelas Borjuasi dan Negara

but they are also daily and hourly enslaved by the machine

tetapi mereka juga diperhambakan setiap hari dan setiap jam oleh mesin

they are enslaved by the over-looker, and, above all, by the individual Bourgeoisie manufacturer himself

mereka diperhambakan oleh pemerhati, dan, di atas semua, oleh pengilang Borjuasi individu itu sendiri

The more openly this despotism proclaims gain to be its end and aim, the more petty, the more hateful and the more embittering it is

Semakin terbuka despotisme ini mengisytiharkan keuntungan sebagai akhir dan matlamatnya, semakin kecil, semakin benci dan semakin pahit

the more modern industry becomes developed, the lesser are the differences between the sexes

semakin industri moden menjadi maju, semakin kecil perbezaan antara jantina

The less the skill and exertion of strength implied in manual labour, the more is the labour of men superseded by that of women

Semakin kurang kemahiran dan usaha kekuatan yang tersirat dalam buruh manual, semakin banyak buruh lelaki digantikan oleh buruh wanita

Differences of age and sex no longer have any distinctive social validity for the working class

Perbezaan umur dan jantina tidak lagi mempunyai kesahihan sosial yang tersendiri untuk kelas pekerja

All are instruments of labour, more or less expensive to use, according to their age and sex

Semua adalah alat buruh, lebih kurang mahal untuk digunakan, mengikut umur dan jantina mereka

as soon as the labourer receives his wages in cash, than he is set upon by the other portions of the Bourgeoisie

sebaik sahaja buruh menerima upahnya secara tunai, daripada dia ditetapkan oleh bahagian-bahagian Borjuasi yang lain

the landlord, the shopkeeper, the pawnbroker, etc

tuan tanah, penjaga kedai, pajak gadai, dll

The lower strata of the middle class; the small trades people and shopkeepers

Lapisan bawah kelas pertengahan; peniaga kecil orang dan pekedai

the retired tradesmen generally, and the handicraftsmen and peasants

peniaga yang telah bersara secara amnya, dan tukang tangan dan petani

all these sink gradually into the Proletariat

semua ini tenggelam secara beransur-ansur ke dalam Proletariat

partly because their diminutive capital does not suffice for the scale on which Modern Industry is carried on

sebahagiannya kerana modal kecil mereka tidak mencukupi untuk skala di mana Industri Moden dijalankan

and because it is swamped in the competition with the large capitalists

dan kerana ia dibanjiri dalam persaingan dengan kapitalis besar

partly because their specialized skill is rendered worthless by the new methods of production

sebahagiannya kerana kemahiran khusus mereka menjadi tidak bernilai oleh kaedah pengeluaran baru

Thus the Proletariat is recruited from all classes of the population

Oleh itu, Proletariat direkrut daripada semua kelas penduduk

The Proletariat goes through various stages of development

Proletariat melalui pelbagai peringkat pembangunan

With its birth begins its struggle with the Bourgeoisie
Dengan kelahirannya bermula perjuangannya dengan Borjuasi
At first the contest is carried on by individual labourers
Pada mulanya pertandingan dijalankan oleh buruh individu
then the contest is carried on by the workpeople of a factory
Kemudian pertandingan dijalankan oleh pekerja kilang
then the contest is carried on by the operatives of one trade, in one locality
Kemudian pertandingan dijalankan oleh pengendali satu perdagangan, di satu kawasan
and the contest is then against the individual Bourgeoisie who directly exploits them
dan pertandingan itu kemudiannya menentang Borjuasi individu yang mengeksploitasi mereka secara langsung
They direct their attacks not against the Bourgeoisie conditions of production
Mereka mengarahkan serangan mereka bukan terhadap syarat-syarat pengeluaran Borjuasi
but they direct their attack against the instruments of production themselves
tetapi mereka mengarahkan serangan mereka terhadap instrumen pengeluaran itu sendiri
they destroy imported wares that compete with their labour
mereka memusnahkan barangan import yang bersaing dengan buruh mereka
they smash to pieces machinery and they set factories ablaze
mereka menghancurkan jentera dan mereka membakar kilang
they seek to restore by force the vanished status of the workman of the Middle Ages
mereka berusaha untuk memulihkan secara paksa status pekerja Zaman Pertengahan yang lenyap
At this stage the labourers still form an incoherent mass scattered over the whole country
Pada peringkat ini buruh masih membentuk jisim yang tidak koheren yang tersebar di seluruh negara

and they are broken up by their mutual competition
dan mereka dipecahkan oleh persaingan bersama mereka
If anywhere they unite to form more compact bodies, this is not yet the consequence of their own active union
Jika di mana-mana mereka bersatu untuk membentuk badan yang lebih padat, ini belum lagi akibat daripada kesatuan aktif mereka sendiri
but it is a consequence of the union of the Bourgeoisie, to attain its own political ends
tetapi ia adalah akibat daripada penyatuan Borjuasi, untuk mencapai tujuan politiknya sendiri
the Bourgeoisie is compelled to set the whole Proletariat in motion
Borjuasi terpaksa menggerakkan seluruh Proletariat
and moreover, for a time being, the Bourgeoisie is able to do so
dan lebih-lebih lagi, untuk sementara waktu, Borjuasi mampu berbuat demikian
At this stage, therefore, the proletarians do not fight their enemies
Oleh itu, pada peringkat ini, proletar tidak melawan musuh mereka
but instead they are fighting the enemies of their enemies
tetapi sebaliknya mereka melawan musuh musuh mereka
the fight the remnants of absolute monarchy and the landowners
perjuangan sisa-sisa monarki mutlak dan pemilik tanah
they fight the non-industrial Bourgeoisie; the petty Bourgeoisie
mereka melawan Borjuasi bukan perindustrian; Borjuasi kecil
Thus the whole historical movement is concentrated in the hands of the Bourgeoisie
Oleh itu, keseluruhan pergerakan sejarah tertumpu di tangan Borjuasi
every victory so obtained is a victory for the Bourgeoisie

setiap kemenangan yang diperolehi adalah kemenangan bagi
Borjuasi

**But with the development of industry the Proletariat not
only increases in number**

Tetapi dengan perkembangan industri, Proletariat bukan
sahaja meningkat dalam bilangan

**the Proletariat becomes concentrated in greater masses and
its strength grows**

Proletariat menjadi tertumpu dalam jisim yang lebih besar
dan kekuatannya bertambah

and the Proletariat feels that strength more and more

dan Proletariat merasakan kekuatan itu semakin

**The various interests and conditions of life within the ranks
of the Proletariat are more and more equalised**

Pelbagai kepentingan dan keadaan kehidupan dalam barisan
Proletariat semakin disamakan

**they become more in proportion as machinery obliterates all
distinctions of labour**

mereka menjadi lebih berkadaran apabila jentera
melenyapkan semua perbezaan buruh

**and machinery nearly everywhere reduces wages to the same
low level**

dan jentera hampir di mana-mana mengurangkan gaji ke
tahap rendah yang sama

**The growing competition among the Bourgeoisie, and the
resulting commercial crises, make the wages of the workers
ever more fluctuating**

Persaingan yang semakin meningkat di kalangan Borjuasi,
dan krisis komersial yang terhasil, menjadikan gaji pekerja
semakin berubah-ubah

**The unceasing improvement of machinery, ever more
rapidly developing, makes their livelihood more and more
precarious**

Penambahbaikan jentera yang tidak henti-hentinya, semakin
pesat berkembang, menjadikan mata pencarian mereka
semakin tidak menentu

the collisions between individual workmen and individual
Bourgeoisie take more and more the character of collisions
between two classes

perlanggaran antara pekerja individu dan borjuasi individu
mengambil lebih banyak watak perlanggaran antara dua kelas

Thereupon the workers begin to form combinations (Trades
Unions) against the Bourgeoisie

Selepas itu pekerja mula membentuk gabungan (Kesatuan
Sekerja) menentang Borjuasi

they club together in order to keep up the rate of wages

mereka berkumpul bersama untuk mengekalkan kadar upah

they found permanent associations in order to make
provision beforehand for these occasional revolts

mereka menemui persatuan tetap untuk membuat peruntukan
terlebih dahulu untuk pemberontakan sekali-sekala ini

Here and there the contest breaks out into riots

Di sana-sini pertandingan meletus menjadi rusuhan

Now and then the workers are victorious, but only for a time

Kadang-kadang pekerja menang, tetapi hanya untuk seketika

The real fruit of their battles lies, not in the immediate
result, but in the ever-expanding union of the workers

Hasil sebenar pertempuran mereka terletak, bukan pada hasil
serta-merta, tetapi dalam kesatuan pekerja yang sentiasa
berkembang

This union is helped on by the improved means of
communication that are created by modern industry

Kesatuan ini dibantu oleh cara komunikasi yang lebih baik
yang dicipta oleh industri moden

modern communication places the workers of different
localities in contact with one another

komunikasi moden meletakkan pekerja dari kawasan yang
berbeza berhubung antara satu sama lain

It was just this contact that was needed to centralise the
numerous local struggles into one national struggle between
classes

Hanya hubungan inilah yang diperlukan untuk memusatkan banyak perjuangan tempatan ke dalam satu perjuangan nasional antara kelas

all of these struggles are of the same character, and every class struggle is a political struggle

Semua perjuangan ini mempunyai watak yang sama, dan setiap perjuangan kelas adalah perjuangan politik

the burghers of the Middle Ages, with their miserable highways, required centuries to form their unions

penduduk Zaman Pertengahan, dengan lebuh raya mereka yang menyedihkan, memerlukan berabad-abad untuk membentuk kesatuan mereka

the modern proletarians, thanks to railways, achieve their unions within a few years

Proletar moden, terima kasih kepada kereta api, mencapai kesatuan mereka dalam masa beberapa tahun

This organisation of the proletarians into a class consequently formed them into a political party

Organisasi proletar ini ke dalam satu kelas akibatnya membentuk mereka menjadi sebuah parti politik

the political class is continually being upset again by the competition between the workers themselves

kelas politik terus terganggu lagi oleh persaingan antara pekerja itu sendiri

But the political class continues to rise up again, stronger, firmer, mightier

Tetapi kelas politik terus bangkit semula, lebih kuat, lebih tegas, lebih kuat

It compels legislative recognition of particular interests of the workers

Ia memaksa pengiktirafan perundangan terhadap kepentingan tertentu pekerja

it does this by taking advantage of the divisions among the Bourgeoisie itself

ia melakukan ini dengan mengambil kesempatan daripada perpecahan di kalangan Borjuasi itu sendiri

Thus the ten-hours' bill in England was put into law
Oleh itu, rang undang-undang sepuluh jam di England telah dimasukkan ke dalam undang-undang

in many ways the collisions between the classes of the old society further is the course of development of the Proletariat
dalam banyak cara perlanggaran antara kelas-kelas masyarakat lama selanjutnya adalah perjalanan pembangunan Proletariat

The Bourgeoisie finds itself involved in a constant battle
Borjuasi mendapati dirinya terlibat dalam pertempuran berterusan

At first it will find itself involved in a constant battle with the aristocracy
Pada mulanya ia akan mendapati dirinya terlibat dalam pertempuran berterusan dengan bangsawan

later on it will find itself involved in a constant battle with those portions of the Bourgeoisie itself
kemudian ia akan mendapati dirinya terlibat dalam pertempuran berterusan dengan bahagian-bahagian Borjuasi itu sendiri

and their interests will have become antagonistic to the progress of industry
dan kepentingan mereka akan menjadi antagonis kepada kemajuan industri

at all times, their interests will have become antagonistic with the Bourgeoisie of foreign countries
pada setiap masa, kepentingan mereka akan menjadi antagonis dengan Borjuasi negara-negara asing

In all these battles it sees itself compelled to appeal to the Proletariat, and asks for its help
Dalam semua pertempuran ini, ia melihat dirinya terpaksa merayu kepada Proletariat, dan meminta bantuannya

and thus, it will feel compelled to drag it into the political arena

dan dengan itu, ia akan berasa terpaksa menyeretnya ke arena politik

The Bourgeoisie itself, therefore, supplies the Proletariat with its own instruments of political and general education

Oleh itu, Borjuasi itu sendiri membekalkan Proletariat dengan instrumen pendidikan politik dan amnya sendiri

in other words, it furnishes the Proletariat with weapons for fighting the Bourgeoisie

dalam erti kata lain, ia membekalkan Proletariat dengan senjata untuk memerangi Borjuasi

Further, as we have already seen, entire sections of the ruling classes are precipitated into the Proletariat

Selanjutnya, seperti yang telah kita lihat, seluruh bahagian kelas pemerintah diendapkan ke dalam Proletariat

the advance of industry sucks them into the Proletariat

kemajuan industri menyedut mereka ke dalam Proletariat

or, at least, they are threatened in their conditions of existence

atau, sekurang-kurangnya, mereka terancam dalam keadaan kewujudan mereka

These also supply the Proletariat with fresh elements of enlightenment and progress

Ini juga membekalkan Proletariat dengan unsur-unsur pencerahan dan kemajuan yang segar

Finally, in times when the class struggle nears the decisive hour

Akhirnya, pada masa-masa apabila perjuangan kelas menghampiri waktu yang menentukan

the process of dissolution going on within the ruling class

Proses pembubaran yang berlaku dalam kelas pemerintah

in fact, the dissolution going on within the ruling class will be felt within the whole range of society

Malah, pembubaran yang berlaku dalam kelas pemerintah akan dirasai dalam seluruh rangkaian masyarakat

it will take on such a violent, glaring character, that a small section of the ruling class cuts itself adrift

ia akan mengambil watak yang ganas dan mencolok, sehingga sebahagian kecil kelas pemerintah memotong dirinya hanyut

and that ruling class will join the revolutionary class

dan kelas pemerintah itu akan menyertai kelas revolusioner

the revolutionary class being the class that holds the future in its hands

kelas revolusioner menjadi kelas yang memegang masa depan di tangannya

Just as at an earlier period, a section of the nobility went over to the Bourgeoisie

Sama seperti pada tempoh sebelumnya, sebahagian bangsawan beralih kepada Borjuasi

the same way a portion of the Bourgeoisie will go over to the Proletariat

dengan cara yang sama sebahagian daripada Borjuasi akan diserahkan kepada Proletariat

in particular, a portion of the Bourgeoisie will go over to a portion of the Bourgeoisie ideologists

khususnya, sebahagian daripada Borjuasi akan diserahkan kepada sebahagian daripada ideologi Borjuasi

Bourgeoisie ideologists who have raised themselves to the level of comprehending theoretically the historical movement as a whole

Ahli ideologi borjuasi yang telah menaikkan diri mereka ke tahap memahami secara teori pergerakan sejarah secara keseluruhan

Of all the classes that stand face to face with the Bourgeoisie today, the Proletariat alone is a really revolutionary class

Daripada semua kelas yang bersemuka dengan Borjuasi hari ini, Proletariat sahaja adalah kelas yang benar-benar revolusioner

The other classes decay and finally disappear in the face of Modern Industry

Kelas-kelas lain reput dan akhirnya hilang di hadapan Industri Moden

the Proletariat is its special and essential product

Proletariat adalah produk istimewa dan penting

The lower middle class, the small manufacturer, the shopkeeper, the artisan, the peasant

Kelas menengah bawah, pengilang kecil, penjaga kedai, tukang, petani

all these fight against the Bourgeoisie

semua ini berjuang menentang Borjuasi

they fight as fractions of the middle class to save themselves from extinction

mereka berjuang sebagai pecahan kelas menengah untuk menyelamatkan diri mereka daripada kepupusan

They are therefore not revolutionary, but conservative

Oleh itu, mereka tidak revolusioner, tetapi konservatif

Nay more, they are reactionary, for they try to roll back the wheel of history

Lebih-lebih lagi, mereka adalah reaksioner, kerana mereka cuba memutar balik roda sejarah

If by chance they are revolutionary, they are so only in view of their impending transfer into the Proletariat

Jika secara kebetulan mereka revolusioner, mereka begitu hanya memandangkan peralihan mereka yang akan datang ke dalam Proletariat

they thus defend not their present, but their future interests

dengan itu mereka bukan mempertahankan masa kini mereka, tetapi kepentingan masa depan mereka

they desert their own standpoint to place themselves at that of the Proletariat

mereka meninggalkan pendirian mereka sendiri untuk meletakkan diri mereka pada pendirian Proletariat

The "dangerous class," the social scum, that passively rotting mass thrown off by the lowest layers of old society

"Kelas berbahaya", sampah sosial, jisim reput pasif yang dibuang oleh lapisan terendah masyarakat lama

they may, here and there, be swept into the movement by a proletarian revolution

mereka mungkin, di sana-sini, dihanyutkan ke dalam gerakan oleh revolusi proletar

its conditions of life, however, prepare it far more for the part of a bribed tool of reactionary intrigue

keadaan hidupnya, bagaimanapun, menyediakannya lebih banyak untuk bahagian alat tipu daya reaksioner yang disogok

In the conditions of the Proletariat, those of old society at large are already virtually swamped

Dalam keadaan Proletariat, masyarakat lama secara amnya sudah hampir dibanjiri

The proletarian is without property

Proletar tidak mempunyai harta

his relation to his wife and children has no longer anything in common with the Bourgeoisie's family-relations

hubungannya dengan isteri dan anak-anaknya tidak lagi mempunyai apa-apa persamaan dengan hubungan keluarga Borjuasi

modern industrial labour, modern subjection to capital, the same in England as in France, in America as in Germany

buruh perindustrian moden, ketundukan moden kepada modal, sama di England seperti di Perancis, di Amerika seperti di Jerman

his condition in society has stripped him of every trace of national character

keadaannya dalam masyarakat telah melucutkan setiap kesan watak kebangsaan

Law, morality, religion, are to him so many Bourgeoisie prejudices

Undang-undang, moral, agama, baginya begitu banyak prasangka Borjuasi

and behind these prejudices lurk in ambush just as many Bourgeoisie interests

dan di sebalik prasangka ini mengintai dalam serangan hendap sama seperti banyak kepentingan Borjuasi

All the preceding classes that got the upper hand, sought to fortify their already acquired status
Semua kelas terdahulu yang mendapat kelebihan, berusaha untuk mengukuhkan status mereka yang telah diperolehi

they did this by subjecting society at large to their conditions of appropriation
mereka melakukan ini dengan menundukkan masyarakat secara amnya kepada syarat peruntukan mereka

The proletarians cannot become masters of the productive forces of society
Proletar tidak boleh menjadi tuan kepada kuasa produktif masyarakat

it can only do this by abolishing their own previous mode of appropriation
ia hanya boleh melakukan ini dengan memansuhkan cara peruntukan mereka sendiri sebelum ini

and thereby it also abolishes every other previous mode of appropriation
dan dengan itu ia juga memansuhkan setiap cara peruntukan terdahulu yang lain

They have nothing of their own to secure and to fortify
Mereka tidak mempunyai apa-apa untuk dijamin dan diperkuat

their mission is to destroy all previous securities for, and insurances of, individual property
Misi mereka adalah untuk memusnahkan semua sekuriti terdahulu untuk, dan insurans, harta individu

All previous historical movements were movements of minorities
Semua pergerakan sejarah sebelum ini adalah pergerakan minoriti

or they were movements in the interests of minorities
atau mereka adalah pergerakan demi kepentingan minoriti

The proletarian movement is the self-conscious, independent movement of the immense majority

Gerakan proletar ialah gerakan sedar diri dan bebas majoriti besar

and it is a movement in the interests of the immense majority

dan ia adalah pergerakan demi kepentingan majoriti besar

The Proletariat, the lowest stratum of our present society

Proletariat, lapisan terendah dalam masyarakat kita sekarang

it cannot stir or raise itself up without the whole superincumbent strata of official society being sprung into the air

ia tidak boleh menggerakkan atau membangkitkan dirinya tanpa seluruh lapisan penyandang masyarakat rasmi yang muncul ke udara

Though not in substance, yet in form, the struggle of the Proletariat with the Bourgeoisie is at first a national struggle

Walaupun tidak dalam substansi, namun dalam bentuk, perjuangan Proletariat dengan Borjuasi pada mulanya adalah perjuangan nasional

The Proletariat of each country must, of course, first of all settle matters with its own Bourgeoisie

Proletariat setiap negara mesti, tentu saja, terlebih dahulu menyelesaikan perkara dengan Borjuasinya sendiri

In depicting the most general phases of the development of the Proletariat, we traced the more or less veiled civil war

Dalam menggambarkan fasa yang paling umum dalam perkembangan Proletariat, kami mengesan perang saudara yang lebih kurang terselubung

this civil is raging within existing society

sivil ini berkecamuk dalam masyarakat sedia ada

it will rage up to the point where that war breaks out into open revolution

ia akan berkecamuk sehingga ke tahap di mana perang itu meletus menjadi revolusi terbuka

and then the violent overthrow of the Bourgeoisie lays the foundation for the sway of the Proletariat

dan kemudian penggulingan Borjuasi yang ganas meletakkan asas untuk pengaruh Proletariat

Hitherto, every form of society has been based, as we have already seen, on the antagonism of oppressing and oppressed classes

Sehingga kini, setiap bentuk masyarakat telah berdasarkan, seperti yang telah kita lihat, pada antagonisme kelas yang menindas dan ditindas

But in order to oppress a class, certain conditions must be assured to it

Tetapi untuk menindas kelas, syarat-syarat tertentu mesti dijamin kepadanya

the class must be kept under conditions in which it can, at least, continue its slavish existence

kelas mesti disimpan di bawah keadaan di mana ia boleh, sekurang-kurangnya, meneruskan kewujudannya yang seperti hamba

The serf, in the period of serfdom, raised himself to membership in the commune

Hamba, dalam tempoh perhambaan, menaikkan dirinya kepada keahlian dalam komune

just as the petty Bourgeoisie, under the yoke of feudal absolutism, managed to develop into a Bourgeoisie

sama seperti Borjuasi kecil, di bawah kuk absolutisme feudal, berjaya berkembang menjadi Borjuasi

The modern labourer, on the contrary, instead of rising with the progress of industry, sinks deeper and deeper

Buruh moden, sebaliknya, bukannya bangkit dengan kemajuan industri, tenggelam lebih dalam dan lebih dalam

he sinks below the conditions of existence of his own class

dia tenggelam di bawah syarat kewujudan kelasnya sendiri

He becomes a pauper, and pauperism develops more rapidly than population and wealth

Dia menjadi orang miskin, dan kemiskinan berkembang lebih cepat daripada penduduk dan kekayaan

And here it becomes evident, that the Bourgeoisie is unfit any longer to be the ruling class in society

Dan di sini menjadi jelas, bahawa Borjuasi tidak lagi layak untuk menjadi kelas pemerintah dalam masyarakat

and it is unfit to impose its conditions of existence upon society as an over-riding law

dan adalah tidak sesuai untuk mengenakan syarat-syarat kewujudannya ke atas masyarakat sebagai undang-undang yang mengatasi

It is unfit to rule because it is incompetent to assure an existence to its slave within his slavery

Ia tidak layak untuk memerintah kerana ia tidak cekap untuk menjamin kewujudan kepada hambanya dalam perhambaannya

because it cannot help letting him sink into such a state, that it has to feed him, instead of being fed by him

kerana ia tidak dapat membantu membiarkannya tenggelam ke dalam keadaan sedemikian, sehingga ia perlu memberinya makan, bukannya diberi makan olehnya

Society can no longer live under this Bourgeoisie

Masyarakat tidak lagi boleh hidup di bawah Borjuasi ini

in other words, its existence is no longer compatible with society

Dalam erti kata lain, kewujudannya tidak lagi serasi dengan masyarakat

The essential condition for the existence, and for the sway of the Bourgeoisie class, is the formation and augmentation of capital

Syarat penting untuk kewujudan, dan untuk pengaruh kelas Borjuasi, ialah pembentukan dan penambahan modal

the condition for capital is wage-labour

Syarat untuk modal ialah buruh upah

Wage-labour rests exclusively on competition between the labourers

Buruh upah terletak secara eksklusif pada persaingan antara buruh

The advance of industry, whose involuntary promoter is the Bourgeoisie, replaces the isolation of the labourers

Kemajuan industri, yang penganjur sukarelanya ialah Borjuasi, menggantikan pengasingan buruh

due to competition, due to their revolutionary combination, due to association

kerana persaingan, kerana gabungan revolusioner mereka, kerana persatuan

The development of Modern Industry cuts from under its feet the very foundation on which the Bourgeoisie produces and appropriates products

Perkembangan Industri Moden memotong dari bawah kakinya asas di mana Borjuasi menghasilkan dan memperuntukkan produk

What the Bourgeoisie produces, above all, is its own grave-diggers

Apa yang dihasilkan oleh Borjuasi, di atas segalanya, ialah penggali kuburnya sendiri

The fall of the Bourgeoisie and the victory of the Proletariat are equally inevitable

Kejatuhan Borjuasi dan kemenangan Proletariat adalah sama tidak dapat dielakkan

Proletarians and Communists
Proletar dan Komunis

In what relation do the Communists stand to the proletarians as a whole?

Dalam hubungan apakah Komunis berdiri dengan proletar secara keseluruhan?

The Communists do not form a separate party opposed to other working-class parties

Komunis tidak membentuk parti berasingan yang menentang parti kelas pekerja yang lain

They have no interests separate and apart from those of the proletariat as a whole

Mereka tidak mempunyai kepentingan yang berasingan dan terpisah daripada kepentingan proletariat secara keseluruhan

They do not set up any sectarian principles of their own, by which to shape and mould the proletarian movement

Mereka tidak menubuhkan apa-apa prinsip mazhab mereka sendiri, yang dengannya untuk membentuk dan membentuk gerakan proletar

The Communists are distinguished from the other working-class parties by only two things

Komunis dibezakan daripada parti kelas pekerja yang lain hanya dengan dua perkara

Firstly, they point out and bring to the front the common interests of the entire proletariat, independently of all nationality

Pertama, mereka menunjukkan dan membawa ke hadapan kepentingan bersama seluruh proletariat, secara bebas daripada semua kewarganegaraan

this they do in the national struggles of the proletarians of the different countries

ini mereka lakukan dalam perjuangan nasional proletar dari negara-negara yang berbeza

Secondly, they always and everywhere represent the interests of the movement as a whole

Kedua, mereka sentiasa dan di mana-mana mewakili kepentingan pergerakan secara keseluruhan

this they do in the various stages of development, which the struggle of the working class against the Bourgeoisie has to pass through

ini mereka lakukan dalam pelbagai peringkat pembangunan, yang perlu dilalui oleh perjuangan kelas pekerja menentang Borjuasi

The Communists, therefore, are on the one hand, practically, the most advanced and resolute section of the working-class parties of every country

Oleh itu, Komunis adalah di satu pihak, secara praktikal, bahagian yang paling maju dan tegas dalam parti-parti kelas pekerja di setiap negara

they are that section of the working class which pushes forward all others

mereka adalah bahagian kelas pekerja yang mendorong semua yang lain

theoretically, they also have the advantage of clearly understanding the line of march

Secara teorinya, mereka juga mempunyai kelebihan untuk memahami dengan jelas garis perarakan

this they understand better compared the great mass of the proletariat

Ini mereka lebih faham berbanding jisim besar proletariat

they understand the conditions, and the ultimate general results of the proletarian movement

mereka memahami keadaan, dan hasil umum muktamad gerakan proletar

The immediate aim of the Communist is the same as that of all the other proletarian parties

Matlamat segera Komunis adalah sama dengan semua parti proletar yang lain

their aim is the formation of the proletariat into a class

matlamat mereka ialah pembentukan proletariat ke dalam kelas

they aim to overthrow the Bourgeoisie supremacy

mereka berhasrat untuk menggulingkan ketuanan Borjuasi

the strive for the conquest of political power by the proletariat

usaha untuk penaklukan kuasa politik oleh proletariat

The theoretical conclusions of the Communists are in no way based on ideas or principles of reformers

Kesimpulan teori Komunis sama sekali tidak berdasarkan idea atau prinsip reformis

it wasn't would-be universal reformers that invented or discovered the theoretical conclusions of the Communists

bukan bakal pembaharu sejagat yang mencipta atau menemui kesimpulan teori Komunis

They merely express, in general terms, actual relations springing from an existing class struggle

Mereka hanya menyatakan, secara umum, hubungan sebenar yang timbul daripada perjuangan kelas yang sedia ada

and they describe the historical movement going on under our very eyes that have created this class struggle

dan mereka menggambarkan pergerakan sejarah yang berlaku di bawah mata kita yang telah mewujudkan perjuangan kelas ini

The abolition of existing property relations is not at all a distinctive feature of Communism

Pemansuhan hubungan harta sedia ada sama sekali bukan ciri khas Komunisme

All property relations in the past have continually been subject to historical change

Semua hubungan harta pada masa lalu terus tertakluk kepada perubahan sejarah

and these changes were consequent upon the change in historical conditions

dan perubahan ini adalah akibat daripada perubahan dalam keadaan sejarah

The French Revolution, for example, abolished feudal property in favour of Bourgeoisie property

Revolusi Perancis, sebagai contoh, memansuhkan harta feudal dan memihak kepada harta Borjuasi

The distinguishing feature of Communism is not the abolition of property, generally

Ciri yang membezakan Komunisme bukanlah pemansuhan harta, secara amnya

but the distinguishing feature of Communism is the abolition of Bourgeoisie property

tetapi ciri yang membezakan Komunisme ialah pemansuhan harta Borjuasi

But modern Bourgeoisie private property is the final and most complete expression of the system of producing and appropriating products

Tetapi harta persendirian Borjuasi moden adalah ungkapan terakhir dan paling lengkap dari sistem menghasilkan dan memperuntukkan produk

it is the final state of a system that is based on class antagonisms, where class antagonism is the exploitation of the many by the few

Ia adalah keadaan akhir sistem yang berdasarkan antagonisme kelas, di mana antagonisme kelas adalah eksploitasi ramai oleh segelintir orang

In this sense, the theory of the Communists may be summed up in the single sentence; the Abolition of private property

Dalam pengertian ini, teori Komunis boleh disimpulkan dalam satu ayat; pemansuhan harta persendirian

We Communists have been reproached with the desire of abolishing the right of personally acquiring property

Kami Komunis telah dicela dengan keinginan untuk memansuhkan hak memperoleh harta secara peribadi

it is claimed that this property is the fruit of a man's own labour

Didakwa bahawa harta ini adalah hasil kerja manusia sendiri

and this property is alleged to be the groundwork of all personal freedom, activity and independence.

dan harta ini didakwa menjadi asas kepada semua kebebasan peribadi, aktiviti dan kemerdekaan.

"Hard-won, self-acquired, self-earned property!"

"Harta yang dimenangi dengan susah payah, diperoleh sendiri, diperoleh sendiri!"

Do you mean the property of the petty artisan and of the small peasant?

Adakah anda maksudkan harta tukang kecil dan petani kecil?

Do you mean a form of property that preceded the Bourgeoisie form?

Adakah anda maksudkan satu bentuk harta yang mendahului bentuk Borjuasi?

There is no need to abolish that, the development of industry has to a great extent already destroyed it

Tidak perlu memansuhkannya, pembangunan industri sebahagian besarnya telah memusnahkannya

and development of industry is still destroying it daily

dan pembangunan industri masih memusnahkannya setiap hari

Or do you mean modern Bourgeoisie private property?

Atau adakah anda maksudkan harta persendirian Borjuasi moden?

But does wage-labour create any property for the labourer?

Tetapi adakah buruh upah mencipta apa-apa harta untuk buruh?

no, wage labour creates not one bit of this kind of property!

Tidak, buruh upah tidak mencipta sedikit pun daripada harta seperti ini!

what wage labour does create is capital; that kind of property which exploits wage-labour

apa yang dicipta oleh buruh upah ialah modal; jenis harta yang mengeksploitasi buruh upah

capital cannot increase except upon condition of begetting a new supply of wage-labour for fresh exploitation

modal tidak boleh meningkat kecuali dengan syarat melahirkan bekalan buruh upah baru untuk eksploitasi baru

Property, in its present form, is based on the antagonism of capital and wage-labour

Harta, dalam bentuknya sekarang, adalah berdasarkan antagonisme modal dan buruh upah

Let us examine both sides of this antagonism

Mari kita periksa kedua-dua belah antagonisme ini

To be a capitalist is to have not only a purely personal status

Menjadi seorang kapitalis bukan sahaja mempunyai status peribadi semata-mata

instead, to be a capitalist is also to have a social status in production

sebaliknya, menjadi kapitalis juga mempunyai status sosial dalam pengeluaran

because capital is a collective product; only by the united action of many members can it be set in motion

kerana modal adalah produk kolektif; Hanya dengan tindakan bersatu ramai ahli boleh digerakkan

but this united action is a last resort, and actually requires all members of society

Tetapi tindakan bersatu ini adalah pilihan terakhir, dan sebenarnya memerlukan semua ahli masyarakat

Capital does get converted into the property of all members of society

Modal memang ditukar kepada harta semua ahli masyarakat

but Capital is, therefore, not a personal power; it is a social power

tetapi Modal, oleh itu, bukan kuasa peribadi; ia adalah kuasa sosial

so when capital is converted into social property, personal property is not thereby transformed into social property

Jadi apabila modal ditukar kepada harta sosial, harta peribadi tidak diubah menjadi harta sosial

It is only the social character of the property that is changed, and loses its class-character

Ia hanya watak sosial harta yang berubah, dan kehilangan watak kelasnya

Let us now look at wage-labour

Sekarang mari kita lihat buruh upah

The average price of wage-labour is the minimum wage, i.e., that quantum of the means of subsistence

Harga purata buruh upah ialah gaji minimum, iaitu, kuantum sara hidup

this wage is absolutely requisite in bare existence as a labourer

Gaji ini benar-benar diperlukan dalam kewujudan kosong sebagai buruh

What, therefore, the wage-labourer appropriates by means of his labour, merely suffices to prolong and reproduce a bare existence

Oleh itu, apa yang diperuntukkan oleh buruh upah melalui kerjanya, hanya mencukupi untuk memanjangkan dan menghasilkan semula kewujudan kosong

We by no means intend to abolish this personal appropriation of the products of labour

Kami sama sekali tidak berhasrat untuk memansuhkan perampasan peribadi produk buruh ini

an appropriation that is made for the maintenance and reproduction of human life

peruntukan yang dibuat untuk penyelenggaraan dan pembiakan kehidupan manusia

such personal appropriation of the products of labour leave no surplus wherewith to command the labour of others

perampasan peribadi produk buruh sedemikian tidak meninggalkan lebihan untuk memerintahkan buruh orang lain

All that we want to do away with, is the miserable character of this appropriation

Apa yang kita mahu hapuskan, ialah watak menyedihkan peruntukan ini

the appropriation under which the labourer lives merely to increase capital

peruntukan di mana buruh hidup semata-mata untuk meningkatkan modal

he is allowed to live only in so far as the interest of the ruling class requires it

dia dibenarkan hidup hanya setakat kepentingan kelas pemerintah memerlukannya

In Bourgeoisie society, living labour is but a means to increase accumulated labour

Dalam masyarakat Borjuasi, buruh hidup hanyalah satu cara untuk meningkatkan buruh terkumpul

In Communist society, accumulated labour is but a means to widen, to enrich, to promote the existence of the labourer

Dalam masyarakat Komunis, buruh terkumpul hanyalah satu cara untuk meluaskan, memperkaya, mempromosikan kewujudan buruh

In Bourgeoisie society, therefore, the past dominates the present

Oleh itu, dalam masyarakat Borjuasi, masa lalu mendominasi masa kini

in Communist society the present dominates the past

dalam masyarakat Komunis masa kini mendominasi masa lalu

In Bourgeoisie society capital is independent and has individuality

Dalam masyarakat borjuasi, modal adalah bebas dan mempunyai keperibadian

In Bourgeoisie society the living person is dependent and has no individuality

Dalam masyarakat Borjuasi, orang yang hidup bergantung dan tidak mempunyai keperibadian

And the abolition of this state of things is called by the Bourgeoisie, abolition of individuality and freedom!

Dan pemansuhan keadaan ini dipanggil oleh Borjuasi, pemansuhan keperibadian dan kebebasan!

And it is rightly called the abolition of individuality and freedom!

Dan ia betul-betul dipanggil pemansuhan keperibadian dan kebebasan!

Communism aims for the abolition of Bourgeoisie individuality

Komunisme bertujuan untuk menghapuskan keperibadian Borjuasi

Communism intends for the abolition of Bourgeoisie independence

Komunisme berhasrat untuk pemansuhan kemerdekaan Borjuasi

Bourgeoisie freedom is undoubtedly what communism is aiming at

Kebebasan borjuasi sudah pasti apa yang disasarkan oleh komunisme

under the present Bourgeoisie conditions of production, freedom means free trade, free selling and buying

di bawah syarat-syarat pengeluaran Borjuasi sekarang, kebebasan bermaksud perdagangan bebas, penjualan dan pembelian bebas

But if selling and buying disappears, free selling and buying also disappears

Tetapi jika jual dan beli hilang, jual dan beli percuma juga hilang

"brave words" by the Bourgeoisie about free selling and buying only have meaning in a limited sense

"kata-kata berani" oleh Borjuasi tentang penjualan dan pembelian percuma hanya mempunyai makna dalam erti kata yang terhad

these words have meaning only in contrast with restricted selling and buying

Perkataan-perkataan ini hanya mempunyai makna berbeza dengan penjualan dan pembelian terhad

and these words have meaning only when applied to the fettered traders of the Middle Ages

dan kata-kata ini hanya mempunyai makna apabila
digunakan kepada pedagang yang terbelenggu pada Zaman
Pertengahan

**and that assumes these words even have meaning in a
Bourgeoisie sense**

dan itu menganggap kata-kata ini mempunyai makna dalam
erti kata Borjuasi

**but these words have no meaning when they're being used
to oppose the Communistic abolition of buying and selling**

tetapi kata-kata ini tidak mempunyai makna apabila ia
digunakan untuk menentang pemansuhan Komunis untuk
membeli dan menjual

**the words have no meaning when they're being used to
oppose the Bourgeoisie conditions of production being
abolished**

perkataan itu tidak mempunyai makna apabila ia digunakan
untuk menentang syarat pengeluaran Borjuasi yang
dimansuhkan

**and they have no meaning when they're being used to
oppose the Bourgeoisie itself being abolished**

dan mereka tidak mempunyai makna apabila mereka
digunakan untuk menentang Borjuasi itu sendiri
dimansuhkan

**You are horrified at our intending to do away with private
property**

Anda ngeri dengan niat kami untuk menghapuskan harta
persendirian

**But in your existing society, private property is already done
away with for nine-tenths of the population**

Tetapi dalam masyarakat sedia ada anda, harta persendirian
telah dihapuskan untuk sembilan persepuluh daripada
penduduk

**the existence of private property for the few is solely due to
its non-existence in the hands of nine-tenths of the
population**

Kewujudan harta persendirian untuk segelintir orang adalah semata-mata kerana ketiadaannya di tangan sembilan persepuluh daripada penduduk

You reproach us, therefore, with intending to do away with a form of property

Oleh itu, anda mencela kami dengan niat untuk menghapuskan satu bentuk harta

but private property necessitates the non-existence of any property for the immense majority of society

tetapi harta persendirian memerlukan ketiadaan apa-apa harta untuk majoriti besar masyarakat

In one word, you reproach us with intending to do away with your property

Dalam satu perkataan, anda mencela kami dengan niat untuk menghapuskan harta benda anda

And it is precisely so; doing away with your Property is just what we intend

Dan memang begitu; menghapuskan Harta anda adalah apa yang kami mahukan

From the moment when labour can no longer be converted into capital, money, or rent

Dari saat buruh tidak lagi boleh ditukar kepada modal, wang, atau sewa

when labour can no longer be converted into a social power capable of being monopolised

apabila buruh tidak lagi boleh ditukar kepada kuasa sosial yang mampu dimonopoli

from the moment when individual property can no longer be transformed into Bourgeoisie property

dari saat apabila harta individu tidak lagi boleh diubah menjadi harta Borjuasi

from the moment when individual property can no longer be transformed into capital

dari saat harta individu tidak lagi boleh diubah menjadi modal

from that moment, you say individuality vanishes

dari saat itu, anda mengatakan keperibadian lenyap

You must, therefore, confess that by "individual" you mean no other person than the Bourgeoisie

Oleh itu, anda mesti mengaku bahawa dengan "individu" anda tidak bermaksud orang lain selain Borjuasi

you must confess it specifically refers to the middle-class owner of property

anda mesti mengaku ia secara khusus merujuk kepada pemilik harta kelas pertengahan

This person must, indeed, be swept out of the way, and made impossible

Orang ini, sememangnya, mesti disapu keluar dari jalan, dan dibuat mustahil

Communism deprives no man of the power to appropriate the products of society

Komunisme tidak melucutkan kuasa manusia untuk mengambil produk masyarakat

all that Communism does is to deprive him of the power to subjugate the labour of others by means of such appropriation

apa yang dilakukan oleh Komunisme adalah untuk melucutkan kuasanya untuk menundukkan kerja orang lain melalui peruntukan sedemikian

It has been objected that upon the abolition of private property all work will cease

Telah dibantah bahawa apabila pemansuhan harta persendirian semua kerja akan dihentikan

and it is then suggested that universal laziness will overtake us

dan kemudian dicadangkan bahawa kemalasan sejagat akan mengatasi kita

According to this, Bourgeoisie society ought long ago to have gone to the dogs through sheer idleness

Menurut ini, masyarakat Borjuasi sepatutnya lama dahulu pergi kepada anjing melalui kemalasan semata-mata

because those of its members who work, acquire nothing

kerana ahli-ahlinya yang bekerja, tidak memperoleh apa-apa

and those of its members who acquire anything, do not work

dan ahli-ahlinya yang memperoleh apa-apa, tidak bekerja

The whole of this objection is but another expression of the tautology

Keseluruhan bantahan ini hanyalah satu lagi ungkapan tautologi

there can no longer be any wage-labour when there is no longer any capital

tidak boleh ada lagi buruh upah apabila tiada lagi modal

there is no difference between material products and mental products

Tiada perbezaan antara produk material dan produk mental

communism proposes both of these are produced in the same way

Komunisme mencadangkan kedua-duanya dihasilkan dengan cara yang sama

but the objections against the Communistic modes of producing these are the same

tetapi bantahan terhadap cara Komunis untuk menghasilkannya adalah sama

to the Bourgeoisie the disappearance of class property is the disappearance of production itself

bagi Borjuasi, kehilangan harta kelas adalah kehilangan pengeluaran itu sendiri

so the disappearance of class culture is to him identical with the disappearance of all culture

jadi kehilangan budaya kelas baginya adalah sama dengan kehilangan semua budaya

That culture, the loss of which he laments, is for the enormous majority a mere training to act as a machine

Budaya itu, kehilangan yang dia keluhkan, bagi sebahagian besar adalah latihan semata-mata untuk bertindak sebagai mesin

Communists very much intend to abolish the culture of Bourgeoisie property

Komunis sangat berhasrat untuk menghapuskan budaya harta borjuasi

But don't wrangle with us so long as you apply the standard of your Bourgeoisie notions of freedom, culture, law, etc

Tetapi jangan bertengkar dengan kami selagi anda menggunakan standard tanggapan Borjuasi anda tentang kebebasan, budaya, undang-undang, dll

Your very ideas are but the outgrowth of the conditions of your Bourgeoisie production and Bourgeoisie property

Idea anda hanyalah hasil daripada keadaan pengeluaran Borjuasi dan harta Borjuasi anda

just as your jurisprudence is but the will of your class made into a law for all

sama seperti perundangan anda hanyalah kehendak kelas anda yang dijadikan undang-undang untuk semua

the essential character and direction of this will are determined by the economical conditions your social class create

Watak dan hala tuju penting ini ditentukan oleh keadaan ekonomi yang dicipta oleh kelas sosial anda

The selfish misconception that induces you to transform social forms into eternal laws of nature and of reason

Salah tanggapan mementingkan diri sendiri yang mendorong anda untuk mengubah bentuk sosial menjadi undang-undang alam dan akal yang kekal

the social forms springing from your present mode of production and form of property

bentuk sosial yang timbul daripada cara pengeluaran dan bentuk harta anda sekarang

historical relations that rise and disappear in the progress of production

hubungan sejarah yang meningkat dan hilang dalam kemajuan pengeluaran

this misconception you share with every ruling class that has preceded you

salah tanggapan ini anda berkongsi dengan setiap kelas
pemerintah yang telah mendahului anda

**What you see clearly in the case of ancient property, what
you admit in the case of feudal property**

Apa yang anda lihat dengan jelas dalam kes harta purba, apa
yang anda akui dalam kes harta feudal

**these things you are of course forbidden to admit in the case
of your own Bourgeoisie form of property**

perkara-perkara ini sudah tentu anda dilarang untuk
mengakui dalam kes bentuk harta Borjuasi anda sendiri

**Abolition of the family! Even the most radical flare up at
this infamous proposal of the Communists**

Pemansuhan keluarga! Malah yang paling radikal menyala
pada cadangan Komunis yang terkenal ini

**On what foundation is the present family, the Bourgeoisie
family, based?**

Atas asas apakah keluarga sekarang, keluarga Borjuasi,
berasaskan?

**the foundation of the present family is based on capital and
private gain**

Asas keluarga sekarang adalah berdasarkan modal dan
keuntungan persendirian

**In its completely developed form this family exists only
among the Bourgeoisie**

Dalam bentuknya yang dibangunkan sepenuhnya, keluarga
ini hanya wujud di kalangan Borjuasi

**this state of things finds its complement in the practical
absence of the family among the proletarians**

keadaan ini menemui pelengkapnya dalam ketiadaan
praktikal keluarga di kalangan proletar

this state of things can be found in public prostitution

keadaan ini boleh didapati dalam pelacuran awam

**The Bourgeoisie family will vanish as a matter of course
when its complement vanishes**

Keluarga Borjuasi akan lenyap sebagai perkara biasa apabila
pelengkapnya lenyap

and both of these will will vanish with the vanishing of capital

dan kedua-dua kehendak ini akan lenyap dengan lenyapnya modal

Do you charge us with wanting to stop the exploitation of children by their parents?

Adakah anda menuduh kami mahu menghentikan eksploitasi kanak-kanak oleh ibu bapa mereka?

To this crime we plead guilty

Untuk jenayah ini kami mengaku bersalah

But, you will say, we destroy the most hallowed of relations, when we replace home education by social education

Tetapi, anda akan berkata, kita memusnahkan hubungan yang paling suci, apabila kita menggantikan pendidikan di rumah dengan pendidikan sosial

is your education not also social? And is it not determined by the social conditions under which you educate?

Adakah pendidikan anda juga tidak sosial? Dan bukankah ia ditentukan oleh keadaan sosial di mana anda mendidik?

by the intervention, direct or indirect, of society, by means of schools, etc.

melalui campur tangan, langsung atau tidak langsung, masyarakat, melalui sekolah, dsb.

The Communists have not invented the intervention of society in education

Komunis tidak mencipta campur tangan masyarakat dalam pendidikan

they do but seek to alter the character of that intervention

mereka hanya berusaha untuk mengubah watak campur tangan itu

and they seek to rescue education from the influence of the ruling class

dan mereka berusaha untuk menyelamatkan pendidikan daripada pengaruh kelas pemerintah

The Bourgeoisie talk of the hallowed co-relation of parent and child

Perbincangan Borjuasi tentang hubungan bersama yang suci
antara ibu bapa dan anak

**but this clap-trap about the family and education becomes
all the more disgusting when we look at Modern Industry**

tetapi perangkap tepukan tentang keluarga dan pendidikan
ini menjadi lebih menjijikkan apabila kita melihat Industri
Moden

**all family ties among the proletarians are torn asunder by
modern industry**

Semua hubungan keluarga di kalangan proletar terkoyak oleh
industri moden

**their children are transformed into simple articles of
commerce and instruments of labour**

anak-anak mereka diubah menjadi barang perdagangan dan
instrumen buruh yang ringkas

**But you Communists would create a community of women,
screams the whole Bourgeoisie in chorus**

Tetapi anda Komunis akan mewujudkan komuniti wanita,
menjerit seluruh Borjuasi dalam korus

**The Bourgeoisie sees in his wife a mere instrument of
production**

Borjuasi melihat dalam isterinya sebagai alat pengeluaran
semata-mata

**He hears that the instruments of production are to be
exploited by all**

Dia mendengar bahawa instrumen pengeluaran akan
dieksploitasi oleh semua

**and, naturally, he can come to no other conclusion than that
the lot of being common to all will likewise fall to women**

dan, secara semula jadi, dia tidak boleh membuat kesimpulan
lain selain bahawa nasib yang biasa kepada semua juga akan
jatuh kepada wanita

**He has not even a suspicion that the real point is to do away
with the status of women as mere instruments of production**

Dia tidak mempunyai syak wasangka bahawa perkara sebenar adalah untuk menghapuskan status wanita sebagai alat pengeluaran semata-mata

For the rest, nothing is more ridiculous than the virtuous indignation of our Bourgeoisie at the community of women

Selebihnya, tidak ada yang lebih tidak masuk akal daripada kemarahan borjuasi kita terhadap komuniti wanita

they pretend it is to be openly and officially established by the Communists

mereka berpura-pura ia ditubuhkan secara terbuka dan rasmi oleh Komunis

The Communists have no need to introduce community of women, it has existed almost from time immemorial

Komunis tidak perlu memperkenalkan komuniti wanita, ia telah wujud hampir sejak dahulu lagi

Our Bourgeoisie are not content with having the wives and daughters of their proletarians at their disposal

Borjuasi kita tidak berpuas hati dengan mempunyai isteri dan anak perempuan proletar mereka di pelupusan mereka

they take the greatest pleasure in seducing each other's wives

mereka sangat senang menggoda isteri masing-masing

and that is not even to speak of common prostitutes

dan itu tidak bercakap tentang pelacur biasa

Bourgeoisie marriage is in reality a system of wives in common

Perkahwinan borjuasi pada hakikatnya adalah sistem isteri yang sama

then there is one thing that the Communists might possibly be reproached with

maka ada satu perkara yang mungkin dicela oleh Komunis

they desire to introduce an openly legalised community of women

mereka berhasrat untuk memperkenalkan komuniti wanita yang disahkan secara terbuka

rather than a hypocritically concealed community of women

bukannya komuniti wanita yang tersembunyi secara munafik

the community of women springing from the system of production

komuniti wanita yang muncul daripada sistem pengeluaran

abolish the system of production, and you abolish the community of women

menghapuskan sistem pengeluaran, dan anda menghapuskan komuniti wanita

both public prostitution is abolished, and private prostitution

kedua-dua pelacuran awam dimansuhkan, dan pelacuran persendirian

The Communists are further more reproached with desiring to abolish countries and nationality

Komunis lebih dicela dengan keinginan untuk memansuhkan negara dan kewarganegaraan

The working men have no country, so we cannot take from them what they have not got

Lelaki pekerja tidak mempunyai negara, jadi kita tidak boleh mengambil daripada mereka apa yang mereka tidak dapat

the proletariat must first of all acquire political supremacy

proletariat mesti terlebih dahulu memperoleh ketuanan politik

the proletariat must rise to be the leading class of the nation

proletariat mesti bangkit menjadi kelas terkemuka negara

the proletariat must constitute itself the nation

proletariat mesti membentuk dirinya sebagai negara

it is, so far, itself national, though not in the Bourgeoisie sense of the word

ia, setakat ini, itu sendiri bersifat nasional, walaupun tidak dalam erti kata Borjuasi

National differences and antagonisms between peoples are daily more and more vanishing

Perbezaan dan permusuhan nasional antara orang-orang semakin lenyap setiap hari

owing to the development of the Bourgeoisie, to freedom of commerce, to the world-market

disebabkan oleh perkembangan Borjuasi, kebebasan perdagangan, kepada pasaran dunia

to uniformity in the mode of production and in the conditions of life corresponding thereto

kepada keseragaman dalam cara pengeluaran dan dalam keadaan kehidupan yang sepadan dengannya

The supremacy of the proletariat will cause them to vanish still faster

Ketuanan proletariat akan menyebabkan mereka lenyap lebih cepat

United action, of the leading civilised countries at least, is one of the first conditions for the emancipation of the proletariat

Tindakan bersatu, sekurang-kurangnya negara-negara bertamadun terkemuka, adalah salah satu syarat pertama untuk pembebasan proletariat

In proportion as the exploitation of one individual by another is put an end to, the exploitation of one nation by another will also be put an end to

Dalam perkadaran apabila eksploitasi satu individu oleh yang lain ditamatkan, eksploitasi satu negara oleh negara lain juga akan ditamatkan

In proportion as the antagonism between classes within the nation vanishes, the hostility of one nation to another will come to an end

Dalam perkadaran apabila permusuhan antara kelas dalam negara lenyap, permusuhan satu negara terhadap negara lain akan berakhir

The charges against Communism made from a religious, a philosophical, and, generally, from an ideological standpoint, are not deserving of serious examination

Tuduhan terhadap Komunisme yang dibuat daripada agama, falsafah, dan, secara amnya, dari sudut ideologi, tidak patut diperiksa secara serius

Does it require deep intuition to comprehend that man's ideas, views and conceptions changes with every change in the conditions of his material existence?

Adakah ia memerlukan intuisi yang mendalam untuk memahami bahawa idea, pandangan dan konsep manusia berubah dengan setiap perubahan dalam keadaan kewujudan materialnya?

is it not obvious that man's consciousness changes when his social relations and his social life changes?

Bukankah jelas bahawa kesedaran manusia berubah apabila hubungan sosial dan kehidupan sosialnya berubah?

What else does the history of ideas prove, than that intellectual production changes its character in proportion as material production is changed?

Apa lagi yang dibuktikan oleh sejarah idea, daripada pengeluaran intelektual mengubah wataknya mengikut perkadaran apabila pengeluaran material diubah?

The ruling ideas of each age have ever been the ideas of its ruling class

Idea yang memerintah setiap zaman pernah menjadi idea kelas pemerintahnya

When people speak of ideas that revolutionise society, they do but express one fact

Apabila orang bercakap tentang idea yang merevolusikan masyarakat, mereka hanya menyatakan satu fakta

within the old society, the elements of a new one have been created

Dalam masyarakat lama, unsur-unsur yang baru telah dicipta

and that the dissolution of the old ideas keeps even pace with the dissolution of the old conditions of existence

dan bahawa pembubaran idea-idea lama selaras dengan pembubaran syarat-syarat lama kewujudan

When the ancient world was in its last throes, the ancient religions were overcome by Christianity

Apabila dunia purba berada dalam pergolakan terakhirnya, agama-agama purba telah dikalahkan oleh agama Kristian

When Christian ideas succumbed in the 18th century to rationalist ideas, feudal society fought its death battle with the then revolutionary Bourgeoisie

Apabila idea-idea Kristian tunduk pada abad ke-18 kepada idea-idea rasionalis, masyarakat feudal berjuang dalam pertempuran mautnya dengan Borjuasi revolusioner ketika itu

The ideas of religious liberty and freedom of conscience merely gave expression to the sway of free competition within the domain of knowledge

Idea kebebasan beragama dan kebebasan hati nurani hanya memberi ekspresi kepada pengaruh persaingan bebas dalam domain pengetahuan

"Undoubtedly," it will be said, "religious, moral, philosophical and juridical ideas have been modified in the course of historical development"

"Tidak dinafikan," akan dikatakan, "idea-idea agama, moral, falsafah dan perundangan telah diubah suai dalam perjalanan perkembangan sejarah"

"But religion, morality philosophy, political science, and law, constantly survived this change"

"Tetapi agama, falsafah moral, sains politik, dan undang-undang, sentiasa terselamat daripada perubahan ini"

"There are also eternal truths, such as Freedom, Justice, etc"

"Terdapat juga kebenaran abadi, seperti Kebebasan, Keadilan, dll"

"these eternal truths are common to all states of society"

"Kebenaran kekal ini adalah perkara biasa bagi semua keadaan masyarakat"

"But Communism abolishes eternal truths, it abolishes all religion, and all morality"

"Tetapi Komunisme menghapuskan kebenaran abadi, ia menghapuskan semua agama, dan semua moral"

"it does this instead of constituting them on a new basis"

"Ia melakukan ini dan bukannya membentuk mereka secara baharu"

"it therefore acts in contradiction to all past historical experience"

"Oleh itu, ia bertindak bercanggah dengan semua pengalaman sejarah masa lalu"

What does this accusation reduce itself to?

Apakah tuduhan ini mengurangkan dirinya sendiri?

The history of all past society has consisted in the development of class antagonisms

Sejarah semua masyarakat masa lalu telah terdiri daripada perkembangan antagonisme kelas

antagonisms that assumed different forms at different epochs

antagonisme yang mengambil bentuk yang berbeza pada zaman yang berbeza

But whatever form they may have taken, one fact is common to all past ages

Tetapi apa jua bentuk yang mereka ambil, satu fakta adalah biasa untuk semua zaman lampau

the exploitation of one part of society by the other

eksploitasi satu bahagian masyarakat oleh yang lain

No wonder, then, that the social consciousness of past ages moves within certain common forms, or general ideas

Oleh itu, tidak hairanlah bahawa kesedaran sosial zaman lampau bergerak dalam bentuk umum tertentu, atau idea umum

(and that is despite all the multiplicity and variety it displays)

(dan itu walaupun semua kepelbagaian dan kepelbagaian yang dipaparkannya)

and these cannot completely vanish except with the total disappearance of class antagonisms

dan ini tidak boleh lenyap sepenuhnya kecuali dengan hilangnya antagonisme kelas

The Communist revolution is the most radical rupture with traditional property relations

Revolusi Komunis adalah perpecahan paling radikal dengan hubungan harta tradisional

no wonder that its development involves the most radical rupture with traditional ideas

Tidak hairanlah bahawa perkembangannya melibatkan perpecahan paling radikal dengan idea-idea tradisional

But let us have done with the Bourgeoisie objections to Communism

Tetapi marilah kita selesai dengan bantahan Borjuasi terhadap Komunisme

We have seen above the first step in the revolution by the working class

Kita telah melihat di atas langkah pertama dalam revolusi oleh kelas pekerja

proletariat has to be raised to the position of ruling, to win the battle of democracy

proletariat perlu dinaikkan ke kedudukan memerintah, untuk memenangi pertempuran demokrasi

The proletariat will use its political supremacy to wrest, by degrees, all capital from the Bourgeoisie

Proletariat akan menggunakan ketuanan politiknya untuk merampas, secara berperingkat, semua modal daripada Borjuasi

it will centralise all instruments of production in the hands of the State

ia akan memusatkan semua instrumen pengeluaran di tangan Negara

in other words, the proletariat organised as the ruling class

Dalam erti kata lain, proletariat dianjurkan sebagai kelas pemerintah

and it will increase the total of productive forces as rapidly as possible

dan ia akan meningkatkan jumlah daya produktif secepat mungkin

Of course, in the beginning, this cannot be effected except by means of despotic inroads on the rights of property

Sudah tentu, pada mulanya, ini tidak boleh dilaksanakan kecuali melalui pencerobohan zalim terhadap hak harta

and it has to be achieved on the conditions of Bourgeoisie production

dan ia perlu dicapai atas syarat-syarat pengeluaran Borjuasi

it is achieved by means of measures, therefore, which appear economically insufficient and untenable

ia dicapai melalui langkah-langkah, oleh itu, yang kelihatan tidak mencukupi dari segi ekonomi dan tidak dapat dipertahankan

but these means, in the course of the movement, outstrip themselves

tetapi ini bermakna, dalam perjalanan pergerakan, mengatasi diri mereka sendiri

they necessitate further inroads upon the old social order

mereka memerlukan pencerobohan lebih lanjut ke atas tatanan sosial lama

and they are unavoidable as a means of entirely revolutionising the mode of production

dan mereka tidak dapat dielakkan sebagai cara untuk merevolusikan sepenuhnya cara pengeluaran

These measures will of course be different in different countries

Langkah-langkah ini sudah tentu berbeza di negara yang berbeza

Nevertheless in the most advanced countries, the following will be pretty generally applicable

Namun begitu, di negara-negara yang paling maju, perkara berikut akan berlaku secara umum

1. Abolition of property in land and application of all rents of land to public purposes.

1. Pemansuhan harta tanah dan penggunaan semua sewa tanah untuk tujuan awam.

2. A heavy progressive or graduated income tax.

2. Cukai pendapatan progresif atau bergraduat yang berat.

3. Abolition of all right of inheritance.

3. Pemansuhan semua hak warisan.

4. Confiscation of the property of all emigrants and rebels.

4. Rampasan harta semua pendatang dan pemberontak.

5. Centralisation of credit in the hands of the State, by means of a national bank with State capital and an exclusive monopoly.

5. Pemusatan kredit di tangan Negara, melalui bank negara dengan modal Negara dan monopoli eksklusif.

6. Centralisation of the means of communication and transport in the hands of the State.

6. Pemusatan alat komunikasi dan pengangkutan di tangan Negara.

7. Extension of factories and instruments of production owned by the State

7. Peluasan kilang dan instrumen pengeluaran yang dimiliki oleh Kerajaan Negeri

the bringing into cultivation of waste-lands, and the improvement of the soil generally in accordance with a common plan.

membawa ke dalam penanaman tanah terbiar, dan penambahbaikan tanah secara amnya mengikut rancangan bersama.

8. Equal liability of all to labour

8. Liabiliti yang sama semua kepada buruh

Establishment of industrial armies, especially for agriculture.

Penubuhan tentera perindustrian, terutamanya untuk pertanian.

9. Combination of agriculture with manufacturing industries

9. Gabungan pertanian dengan industri pembuatan

gradual abolition of the distinction between town and country, by a more equable distribution of the population over the country.

pemansuhan secara beransur-ansur perbezaan antara bandar dan desa, dengan pengagihan penduduk yang lebih sama rata di seluruh negara.

10. Free education for all children in public schools.
10. Pendidikan percuma untuk semua kanak-kanak di sekolah awam.

Abolition of children's factory labour in its present form
Pemansuhan buruh kilang kanak-kanak dalam bentuknya sekarang

Combination of education with industrial production
Gabungan pendidikan dengan pengeluaran perindustrian

When, in the course of development, class distinctions have disappeared
Apabila, dalam perjalanan pembangunan, perbezaan kelas telah hilang

and when all production has been concentrated in the hands of a vast association of the whole nation
dan apabila semua pengeluaran telah tertumpu di tangan persatuan yang luas seluruh negara

then the public power will lose its political character
maka kuasa awam akan kehilangan watak politiknya

Political power, properly so called, is merely the organised power of one class for oppressing another
Kuasa politik, yang dipanggil, hanyalah kuasa tersusun satu kelas untuk menindas yang lain

If the proletariat during its contest with the Bourgeoisie is compelled, by the force of circumstances, to organise itself as a class
Jika proletariat semasa persaingannya dengan Borjuasi terpaksa, oleh kuasa keadaan, untuk mengatur dirinya sebagai sebuah kelas

if, by means of a revolution, it makes itself the ruling class
jika, melalui revolusi, ia menjadikan dirinya kelas pemerintah

and, as such, it sweeps away by force the old conditions of production
dan, oleh itu, ia menyapu secara paksa keadaan pengeluaran lama

then it will, along with these conditions, have swept away the conditions for the existence of class antagonisms and of classes generally

maka ia akan, bersama-sama dengan syarat-syarat ini, telah menyapu bersih syarat-syarat untuk kewujudan antagonisme kelas dan kelas secara amnya

and will thereby have abolished its own supremacy as a class.

dan dengan itu akan menghapuskan ketuanannya sendiri sebagai sebuah kelas.

In place of the old Bourgeoisie society, with its classes and class antagonisms, we shall have an association

Sebagai ganti masyarakat Borjuasi lama, dengan kelas dan antagonisme kelasnya, kita akan mempunyai persatuan

an association in which the free development of each is the condition for the free development of all

persatuan di mana pembangunan bebas masing-masing adalah syarat untuk pembangunan bebas semua

1) Reactionary Socialism
1) Sosialisme Reaksioner

a) Feudal Socialism
a) Sosialisme Feudal

the aristocracies of France and England had a unique historical position
bangsawan Perancis dan England mempunyai kedudukan sejarah yang unik

it became their vocation to write pamphlets against modern Bourgeoisie society
ia menjadi kerjaya mereka untuk menulis risalah menentang masyarakat Borjuasi moden

In the French revolution of July 1830, and in the English reform agitation
Dalam revolusi Perancis pada Julai 1830, dan dalam pergolakan pembaharuan Inggeris

these aristocracies again succumbed to the hateful upstart
bangsawan ini sekali lagi tunduk kepada pemula yang penuh kebencian

Thenceforth, a serious political contest was altogether out of the question
Sejak itu, pertandingan politik yang serius sama sekali tidak boleh dipersoalkan

All that remained possible was literary battle, not an actual battle
Apa yang mungkin hanyalah pertempuran sastera, bukan pertempuran sebenar

But even in the domain of literature the old cries of the restoration period had become impossible
Tetapi walaupun dalam domain kesusasteraan, tangisan lama tempoh pemulihan telah menjadi mustahil

In order to arouse sympathy, the aristocracy were obliged to lose sight, apparently, of their own interests

Untuk membangkitkan simpati, bangsawan terpaksa kehilangan pandangan, nampaknya, kepentingan mereka sendiri

and they were obliged to formulate their indictment against the Bourgeoisie in the interest of the exploited working class

dan mereka diwajibkan untuk merumuskan dakwaan mereka terhadap Borjuasi demi kepentingan kelas pekerja yang dieksploitasi

Thus the aristocracy took their revenge by singing lampoons on their new master

Oleh itu, golongan bangsawan membalas dendam dengan menyanyikan lampoon pada tuan baru mereka

and they took their revenge by whispering in his ears sinister prophecies of coming catastrophe

dan mereka membalas dendam dengan membisikkan di telinganya ramalan jahat tentang malapetaka yang akan datang

In this way arose Feudal Socialism: half lamentation, half lampoon

Dengan cara ini timbul Sosialisme Feudal: separuh ratapan, separuh lampoon

it rung as half echo of the past, and projected half menace of the future

ia berbunyi sebagai separuh gema masa lalu, dan mengunjurkan separuh ancaman masa depan

at times, by its bitter, witty and incisive criticism, it struck the Bourgeoisie to the very heart's core

kadang-kadang, dengan kritikannya yang pahit, lucu dan tajam, ia menyerang Borjuasi ke teras hati

but it was always ludicrous in its effect, through total incapacity to comprehend the march of modern history

tetapi ia sentiasa menggelikan dalam kesannya, melalui ketidakupayaan total untuk memahami perarakan sejarah moden

The aristocracy, in order to rally the people to them, waved the proletarian alms-bag in front for a banner

Bangsawan, untuk mengumpulkan rakyat kepada mereka, melambai-lambaikan beg sedekah proletar di hadapan untuk sepanduk

But the people, so often as it joined them, saw on their hindquarters the old feudal coats of arms

Tetapi rakyat, begitu kerap menyertai mereka, melihat di bahagian belakang mereka jata feudal lama

and they deserted with loud and irreverent laughter

dan mereka meninggalkan dengan ketawa yang kuat dan tidak sopan

One section of the French Legitimists and "Young England" exhibited this spectacle

Satu bahagian Legitimis Perancis dan "England Muda" mempamerkan tontonan ini

the feudalists pointed out that their mode of exploitation was different to that of the Bourgeoisie

feudalis menunjukkan bahawa cara eksploitasi mereka berbeza dengan Borjuasi

the feudalists forget that they exploited under circumstances and conditions that were quite different

Feudalis lupa bahawa mereka mengeksploitasi dalam keadaan dan keadaan yang agak berbeza

and they didn't notice such methods of exploitation are now antiquated

dan mereka tidak perasan kaedah eksploitasi sedemikian kini sudah lapuk

they showed that, under their rule, the modern proletariat never existed

mereka menunjukkan bahawa, di bawah pemerintahan mereka, proletariat moden tidak pernah wujud

but they forget that the modern Bourgeoisie is the necessary offspring of their own form of society

tetapi mereka lupa bahawa Borjuasi moden adalah keturunan yang diperlukan dalam bentuk masyarakat mereka sendiri

For the rest, they hardly conceal the reactionary character of their criticism

Selebihnya, mereka hampir tidak menyembunyikan watak reaksioner kritikan mereka

their chief accusation against the Bourgeoisie amounts to the following

tuduhan utama mereka terhadap Borjuasi berjumlah seperti berikut

under the Bourgeoisie regime a social class is being developed

di bawah rejim Borjuasi, kelas sosial sedang dibangunkan

this social class is destined to cut up root and branch the old order of society

Kelas sosial ini ditakdirkan untuk memotong akar dan bercabang susunan lama masyarakat

What they upbraid the Bourgeoisie with is not so much that it creates a proletariat

Apa yang mereka kecewa dengan Borjuasi tidak begitu banyak sehingga ia mewujudkan proletariat

what they upbraid the Bourgeoisie with is moreso that it creates a revolutionary proletariat

apa yang mereka tegur dengan Borjuasi lebih-lebih lagi ia mewujudkan proletariat revolusioner

In political practice, therefore, they join in all coercive measures against the working class

Oleh itu, dalam amalan politik, mereka menyertai semua langkah paksaan terhadap kelas pekerja

and in ordinary life, despite their highfalutin phrases, they stoop to pick up the golden apples dropped from the tree of industry

dan dalam kehidupan biasa, walaupun frasa mereka tinggi, mereka membungkuk untuk mengambil epal emas yang dijatuhkan dari pokok industri

and they barter truth, love, and honour for commerce in wool, beetroot-sugar, and potato spirits

dan mereka menukar kebenaran, cinta, dan kehormatan untuk perdagangan dalam bulu, gula bit, dan semangat kentang

As the parson has ever gone hand in hand with the landlord, so has Clerical Socialism with Feudal Socialism

Oleh kerana pendeta pernah seiring dengan tuan tanah, begitu juga dengan Sosialisme Perkeranian dengan Sosialisme Feudal

Nothing is easier than to give Christian asceticism a Socialist tinge

Tiada yang lebih mudah daripada memberikan pertapaan Kristian warna Sosialis

Has not Christianity declaimed against private property, against marriage, against the State?

Bukankah agama Kristian mendakwa terhadap harta persendirian, menentang perkahwinan, terhadap Negara?

Has Christianity not preached in the place of these, charity and poverty?

Bukankah agama Kristian berkhotbah di tempat ini, amal dan kemiskinan?

Does Christianity not preach celibacy and mortification of the flesh, monastic life and Mother Church?

Adakah agama Kristian tidak mengajarkan bujang dan penghinaan daging, kehidupan monastik dan Gereja Ibu?

Christian Socialism is but the holy water with which the priest consecrates the heart-burnings of the aristocrat

Sosialisme Kristian hanyalah air suci yang dengannya imam menguduskan pembakaran hati bangsawan

b) Petty-Bourgeois Socialism
b) Sosialisme Borjuis Kecil

The feudal aristocracy was not the only class that was ruined by the Bourgeoisie
Bangsawan feudal bukan satu-satunya kelas yang dimusnahkan oleh Borjuasi
it was not the only class whose conditions of existence pined and perished in the atmosphere of modern Bourgeoisie society
ia bukan satu-satunya kelas yang keadaan kewujudannya terjepit dan binasa dalam suasana masyarakat Borjuasi moden
The medieval burgesses and the small peasant proprietors were the precursors of the modern Bourgeoisie
Burgesses zaman pertengahan dan pemilik petani kecil adalah pelopor Borjuasi moden
In those countries which are but little developed, industrially and commercially, these two classes still vegetate side by side
Di negara-negara yang kurang maju, dari segi perindustrian dan komersial, kedua-dua kelas ini masih tumbuh-tumbuhan bersebelahan
and in the meantime the Bourgeoisie rise up next to them: industrially, commercially, and politically
dan sementara itu Borjuasi bangkit di sebelah mereka: dari segi perindustrian, komersial, dan politik
In countries where modern civilisation has become fully developed, a new class of petty Bourgeoisie has been formed
Di negara-negara di mana tamadun moden telah berkembang sepenuhnya, kelas baru Borjuasi kecil telah dibentuk
this new social class fluctuates between proletariat and Bourgeoisie
kelas sosial baru ini berubah-ubah antara proletariat dan borjuasi
and it is ever renewing itself as a supplementary part of Bourgeoisie society

dan ia sentiasa memperbaharui dirinya sebagai bahagian
tambahan masyarakat Borjuasi

**The individual members of this class, however, are being
constantly hurled down into the proletariat**

Ahli-ahli individu kelas ini, bagaimanapun, sentiasa
dilemparkan ke dalam proletariat

**they are sucked up by the proletariat through the action of
competition**

mereka disedut oleh proletariat melalui tindakan persaingan

**as modern industry develops they even see the moment
approaching when they will completely disappear as an
independent section of modern society**

Apabila industri moden berkembang, mereka juga melihat
masa yang semakin hampir, apabila mereka akan hilang
sepenuhnya sebagai bahagian bebas masyarakat moden

**they will be replaced, in manufactures, agriculture and
commerce, by overlookers, bailiffs and shopmen**

Mereka akan digantikan, dalam pembuatan, pertanian dan
perdagangan, oleh pemerhati, bailif dan tukang kedai

**In countries like France, where the peasants constitute far
more than half of the population**

Di negara-negara seperti Perancis, di mana petani membentuk
lebih daripada separuh daripada penduduk

**it was natural that there there are writers who sided with the
proletariat against the Bourgeoisie**

adalah wajar bahawa terdapat penulis yang memihak kepada
proletariat menentang Borjuasi

**in their criticism of the Bourgeoisie regime they used the
standard of the peasant and petty Bourgeoisie**

dalam kritikan mereka terhadap rejim Borjuasi, mereka
menggunakan standard petani dan Borjuasi kecil

**and from the standpoint of these intermediate classes they
take up the cudgels for the working class**

dan dari sudut kelas perantaraan ini mereka mengambil
tongkat untuk kelas pekerja

Thus arose petty-Bourgeoisie Socialism, of which Sismondi was the head of this school, not only in France but also in England

Oleh itu, timbul Sosialisme Borjuasi kecil, di mana Sismondi adalah ketua sekolah ini, bukan sahaja di Perancis tetapi juga di England

This school of Socialism dissected with great acuteness the contradictions in the conditions of modern production

Sekolah Sosialisme ini membedah dengan sangat tajam percanggahan dalam keadaan pengeluaran moden

This school laid bare the hypocritical apologies of economists

Sekolah ini mendedahkan permohonan maaf hipokrit ahli ekonomi

This school proved, incontrovertibly, the disastrous effects of machinery and division of labour

Sekolah ini membuktikan, tidak dapat dipertikaikan, kesan bencana jentera dan pembahagian kerja

it proved the concentration of capital and land in a few hands

ia membuktikan penumpuan modal dan tanah di beberapa tangan

it proved how overproduction leads to Bourgeoisie crises

ia membuktikan bagaimana pengeluaran berlebihan membawa kepada krisis Borjuasi

it pointed out the inevitable ruin of the petty Bourgeoisie and peasant

ia menunjukkan kemusnahan yang tidak dapat dielakkan daripada Borjuasi kecil dan petani

the misery of the proletariat, the anarchy in production, the crying inequalities in the distribution of wealth

kesengsaraan proletariat, anarki dalam pengeluaran, ketidaksamaan yang menangis dalam pengagihan kekayaan

it showed how the system of production leads the industrial war of extermination between nations

Ia menunjukkan bagaimana sistem pengeluaran mengetuai perang perindustrian pemusnahan antara negara

the dissolution of old moral bonds, of the old family relations, of the old nationalities

pembubaran ikatan moral lama, hubungan keluarga lama, kewarganegaraan lama

In its positive aims, however, this form of Socialism aspires to achieve one of two things

Walau bagaimanapun, dalam matlamat positifnya, bentuk Sosialisme ini bercita-cita untuk mencapai salah satu daripada dua perkara

either it aims to restore the old means of production and of exchange

sama ada ia bertujuan untuk memulihkan cara pengeluaran dan pertukaran lama

and with the old means of production it would restore the old property relations, and the old society

dan dengan alat pengeluaran lama ia akan memulihkan hubungan harta lama, dan masyarakat lama

or it aims to cramp the modern means of production and exchange into the old framework of the property relations

atau ia bertujuan untuk mengecilkan cara pengeluaran dan pertukaran moden ke dalam rangka kerja lama hubungan harta

In either case, it is both reactionary and Utopian

Dalam kedua-dua kes, ia adalah reaksioner dan Utopia

Its last words are: corporate guilds for manufacture, patriarchal relations in agriculture

Kata-kata terakhirnya ialah: persatuan korporat untuk pembuatan, hubungan patriarki dalam pertanian

Ultimately, when stubborn historical facts had dispersed all intoxicating effects of self-deception

Akhirnya, apabila fakta sejarah yang degil telah menyebarkan semua kesan memabukkan penipuan diri

this form of Socialism ended in a miserable fit of pity

bentuk Sosialisme ini berakhir dengan rasa kasihan yang
menyedihkan

c) German, or "True," Socialism
c) Sosialisme Jerman, atau "Benar"

**The Socialist and Communist literature of France originated
under the pressure of a Bourgeoisie in power**
Kesusasteraan Sosialis dan Komunis Perancis berasal di
bawah tekanan Borjuasi yang berkuasa
**and this literature was the expression of the struggle against
this power**
dan kesusasteraan ini adalah ungkapan perjuangan
menentang kuasa ini
**it was introduced into Germany at a time when the
Bourgeoisie had just begun its contest with feudal
absolutism**
ia diperkenalkan ke Jerman pada masa Borjuasi baru sahaja
memulakan persaingannya dengan absolutisme feudal
**German philosophers, would-be philosophers, and beaux
esprits, eagerly seized on this literature**
Ahli falsafah Jerman, bakal ahli falsafah, dan beaux esprit,
dengan bersemangat merebut kesusasteraan ini
**but they forgot that the writings immigrated from France
into Germany without bringing the French social conditions
along**
tetapi mereka lupa bahawa tulisan-tulisan itu berhijrah dari
Perancis ke Jerman tanpa membawa keadaan sosial Perancis
**In contact with German social conditions, this French
literature lost all its immediate practical significance**
Dalam hubungan dengan keadaan sosial Jerman,
kesusasteraan Perancis ini kehilangan semua kepentingan
praktikalnya yang segera

and the Communist literature of France assumed a purely literary aspect in German academic circles

dan kesusasteraan Komunis Perancis menganggap aspek sastera semata-mata dalam kalangan akademik Jerman

Thus, the demands of the first French Revolution were nothing more than the demands of "Practical Reason"

Oleh itu, tuntutan Revolusi Perancis pertama tidak lebih daripada tuntutan "Alasan Praktikal"

and the utterance of the will of the revolutionary French Bourgeoisie signified in their eyes the law of pure Will

dan ucapan kehendak Borjuasi Perancis yang revolusioner menandakan di mata mereka undang-undang Kehendak murni

it signified Will as it was bound to be; of true human Will generally

ia menandakan Kehendak seperti yang sepatutnya; Kehendak manusia sejati secara amnya

The world of the German literati consisted solely in bringing the new French ideas into harmony with their ancient philosophical conscience

Dunia sasterawan Jerman semata-mata terdiri daripada membawa idea-idea Perancis baru ke dalam harmoni dengan hati nurani falsafah kuno mereka

or rather, they annexed the French ideas without deserting their own philosophic point of view

atau lebih tepatnya, mereka mengilhamkan idea-idea Perancis tanpa meninggalkan sudut pandangan falsafah mereka sendiri

This annexation took place in the same way in which a foreign language is appropriated, namely, by translation

Pengilhakan ini berlaku dengan cara yang sama di mana bahasa asing diperuntukkan, iaitu, melalui terjemahan

It is well known how the monks wrote silly lives of Catholic Saints over manuscripts

Umum mengetahui bagaimana para sami menulis kehidupan bodoh Orang Suci Katolik di atas manuskrip

the manuscripts on which the classical works of ancient heathendom had been written

manuskrip di mana karya-karya klasik kafir kuno telah ditulis

The German literati reversed this process with the profane French literature

Sasterawan Jerman membalikkan proses ini dengan kesusasteraan Perancis yang tidak senonoh

They wrote their philosophical nonsense beneath the French original

Mereka menulis karut falsafah mereka di bawah asal Perancis

For instance, beneath the French criticism of the economic functions of money, they wrote "Alienation of Humanity"

Sebagai contoh, di bawah kritikan Perancis terhadap fungsi ekonomi wang, mereka menulis "Pengasingan Kemanusiaan"

beneath the French criticism of the Bourgeoisie State they wrote "dethronement of the Category of the General"

di bawah kritikan Perancis terhadap Negara Borjuasi mereka menulis "penggulingan Kategori Jeneral"

The introduction of these philosophical phrases at the back of the French historical criticisms they dubbed:

Pengenalan frasa falsafah ini di belakang kritikan sejarah Perancis yang mereka gelarkan:

"Philosophy of Action," "True Socialism," "German Science of Socialism," "Philosophical Foundation of Socialism," and so on

"Falsafah Tindakan," "Sosialisme Sejati," "Sains Sosialisme Jerman," "Asas Falsafah Sosialisme," dan sebagainya

The French Socialist and Communist literature was thus completely emasculated

Oleh itu, kesusasteraan Sosialis dan Komunis Perancis telah dikebiri sepenuhnya

in the hands of the German philosophers it ceased to express the struggle of one class with the other

di tangan ahli falsafah Jerman ia berhenti menyatakan perjuangan satu kelas dengan yang lain

and so the German philosophers felt conscious of having overcome "French one-sidedness"

dan oleh itu ahli falsafah Jerman berasa sedar telah mengatasi "berat sebelah Perancis"

it did not have to represent true requirements, rather, it represented requirements of truth

ia tidak perlu mewakili keperluan sebenar, sebaliknya, ia mewakili keperluan kebenaran

there was no interest in the proletariat, rather, there was interest in Human Nature

tidak ada minat dalam proletariat, sebaliknya, ada minat dalam Sifat Manusia

the interest was in Man in general, who belongs to no class, and has no reality

minatnya adalah pada Manusia secara umum, yang tidak tergolong dalam kelas, dan tidak mempunyai realiti

a man who exists only in the misty realm of philosophical fantasy

seorang lelaki yang hanya wujud dalam alam berkabus fantasi falsafah

but eventually this schoolboy German Socialism also lost its pedantic innocence

tetapi akhirnya budak sekolah Sosialisme Jerman ini juga kehilangan kepolosannya yang bertele-tele

the German Bourgeoisie, and especially the Prussian Bourgeoisie fought against feudal aristocracy

Borjuasi Jerman, dan terutamanya Borjuasi Prusia berjuang menentang bangsawan feudal

the absolute monarchy of Germany and Prussia was also being faught against

monarki mutlak Jerman dan Prusia juga dibantah

and in turn, the literature of the liberal movement also became more earnest

dan seterusnya, kesusasteraan gerakan liberal juga menjadi lebih bersungguh-sungguh

Germany's long wished-for opportunity for "true" Socialism was offered

Peluang Jerman yang telah lama diidam-idamkan untuk Sosialisme "sejati" telah ditawarkan

the opportunity of confronting the political movement with the Socialist demands

peluang untuk menghadapi gerakan politik dengan tuntutan Sosialis

the opportunity of hurling the traditional anathemas against liberalism

peluang untuk melemparkan kutukan tradisional terhadap liberalisme

the opportunity to attack representative government and Bourgeoisie competition

peluang untuk menyerang kerajaan perwakilan dan persaingan Borjuasi

Bourgeoisie freedom of the press, Bourgeoisie legislation, Bourgeoisie liberty and equality

Kebebasan akhbar borjuasi, perundangan borjuasi, kebebasan dan kesaksamaan borjuasi

all of these could now be critiqued in the real world, rather than in fantasy

Semua ini kini boleh dikritik di dunia nyata, dan bukannya dalam fantasi

feudal aristocracy and absolute monarchy had long preached to the masses

Bangsawan feudal dan monarki mutlak telah lama berdakwah kepada orang ramai

"the working man has nothing to lose, and he has everything to gain"

"Lelaki yang bekerja tidak mempunyai apa-apa untuk rugi, dan dia mempunyai segala-galanya untuk diperolehi"

the Bourgeoisie movement also offered a chance to confront these platitudes

gerakan Borjuasi juga menawarkan peluang untuk menghadapi kata-kata kosong ini

the French criticism presupposed the existence of modern
Bourgeoisie society

kritikan Perancis mengandaikan kewujudan masyarakat
Borjuasi moden

Bourgeoisie economic conditions of existence and
Bourgeoisie political constitution

Keadaan kewujudan ekonomi borjuasi dan perlembagaan
politik borjuasi

the very things whose attainment was the object of the
pending struggle in Germany

perkara-perkara yang pencapaiannya menjadi objek
perjuangan yang belum selesai di Jerman

Germany's silly echo of socialism abandoned these goals
just in the nick of time

Gema bodoh Jerman tentang sosialisme meninggalkan
matlamat ini hanya dalam masa yang singkat

the absolute governments had their following of parsons,
professors, country squires and officials

Kerajaan Mutlak mempunyai pengikut mereka daripada
pendeta, profesor, pengawal negara dan pegawai

the government of the time met the German working-class
risings with floggings and bullets

kerajaan pada masa itu menghadapi kebangkitan kelas
pekerja Jerman dengan sebatan dan peluru

for them this socialism served as a welcome scarecrow
against the threatening Bourgeoisie

bagi mereka sosialisme ini berfungsi sebagai orang-orangan
sawah yang dialu-alukan terhadap Borjuasi yang mengancam

and the German government was able to offer a sweet
dessert after the bitter pills it handed out

dan kerajaan Jerman dapat menawarkan pencuci mulut manis
selepas pil pahit yang diberikannya

this "True" Socialism thus served the governments as a
weapon for fighting the German Bourgeoisie

Sosialisme "Sejati" ini dengan itu berkhidmat kepada kerajaan
sebagai senjata untuk memerangi Borjuasi Jerman

and, at the same time, it directly represented a reactionary interest; that of the German Philistines

dan, pada masa yang sama, ia secara langsung mewakili kepentingan reaksioner; iaitu orang Filistin Jerman

In Germany the petty Bourgeoisie class is the real social basis of the existing state of things

Di Jerman, kelas Borjuasi kecil adalah asas sosial sebenar keadaan sedia ada

a relique of the sixteenth century that has constantly been cropping up under various forms

peninggalan abad keenam belas yang sentiasa muncul di bawah pelbagai bentuk

To preserve this class is to preserve the existing state of things in Germany

Untuk memelihara kelas ini adalah untuk mengekalkan keadaan sedia ada di Jerman

The industrial and political supremacy of the Bourgeoisie threatens the petty Bourgeoisie with certain destruction

Ketuanan perindustrian dan politik Borjuasi mengancam Borjuasi kecil dengan kemusnahan tertentu

on the one hand, it threatens to destroy the petty Bourgeoisie through the concentration of capital

di satu pihak, ia mengancam untuk memusnahkan Borjuasi kecil melalui penumpuan modal

on the other hand, the Bourgeoisie threatens to destroy it through the rise of a revolutionary proletariat

sebaliknya, Borjuasi mengancam untuk memusnahkannya melalui kebangkitan proletariat revolusioner

"True" Socialism appeared to kill these two birds with one stone. It spread like an epidemic

Sosialisme "Benar" nampaknya membunuh kedua-dua burung ini dengan satu batu. Ia merebak seperti wabak

The robe of speculative cobwebs, embroidered with flowers of rhetoric, steeped in the dew of sickly sentiment

Jubah sarang labah-labah spekulatif, disulam dengan bunga-bunga retorik, tenggelam dalam embun sentimen yang sakit

this transcendental robe in which the German Socialists wrapped their sorry "eternal truths"

jubah transendental ini di mana Sosialis Jerman membungkus "kebenaran abadi" mereka yang menyedihkan

all skin and bone, served to wonderfully increase the sale of their goods amongst such a public

semua kulit dan tulang, berfungsi untuk meningkatkan penjualan barangan mereka di kalangan orang ramai seperti itu

And on its part, German Socialism recognised, more and more, its own calling

Dan di pihaknya, Sosialisme Jerman mengiktiraf, semakin banyak, panggilannya sendiri

it was called to be the bombastic representative of the petty-Bourgeoisie Philistine

ia dipanggil untuk menjadi wakil bombastik Filistin Borjuis Kecil

It proclaimed the German nation to be the model nation, and German petty Philistine the model man

Ia mengisytiharkan negara Jerman sebagai negara model, dan orang Filistin kecil Jerman sebagai lelaki teladan

To every villainous meanness of this model man it gave a hidden, higher, Socialistic interpretation

Kepada setiap kejahatan jahat lelaki model ini, ia memberikan tafsiran Sosialistik yang tersembunyi, lebih tinggi

this higher, Socialistic interpretation was the exact contrary of its real character

tafsiran Sosialistik yang lebih tinggi ini adalah bertentangan dengan watak sebenar

It went to the extreme length of directly opposing the "brutally destructive" tendency of Communism

Ia pergi ke tahap yang melampau untuk menentang secara langsung kecenderungan Komunisme yang "merosakkan secara kejam"

and it proclaimed its supreme and impartial contempt of all class struggles

dan ia mengisytiharkan penghinaan tertinggi dan tidak berat sebelah terhadap semua perjuangan kelas

With very few exceptions, all the so-called Socialist and Communist publications that now (1847) circulate in Germany belong to the domain of this foul and enervating literature

Dengan sedikit pengecualian, semua penerbitan Sosialis dan Komunis yang kini (1847) beredar di Jerman tergolong dalam domain kesusasteraan yang busuk dan bertenaga ini

2) Conservative Socialism, or Bourgeoisie Socialism
2) Sosialisme Konservatif, atau Sosialisme Borjuasi

A part of the Bourgeoisie is desirous of redressing social grievances
Sebahagian daripada Borjuasi berhasrat untuk membetulkan rungutan sosial

in order to secure the continued existence of Bourgeoisie society
untuk menjamin kewujudan berterusan masyarakat Borjuasi

To this section belong economists, philanthropists, humanitarians
Bahagian ini tergolong ahli ekonomi, dermawan, kemanusiaan

improvers of the condition of the working class and organisers of charity
penambahbaikan keadaan kelas pekerja dan penganjur amal

members of societies for the prevention of cruelty to animals
Ahli Persatuan untuk Pencegahan Kekejaman terhadap Haiwan

temperance fanatics, hole-and-corner reformers of every imaginable kind
fanatik kesederhanaan, pembaharu lubang dan sudut dari setiap jenis yang boleh dibayangkan

This form of Socialism has, moreover, been worked out into complete systems
Bentuk Sosialisme ini, lebih-lebih lagi, telah diusahakan ke dalam sistem yang lengkap

We may cite Proudhon's "Philosophie de la Misère" as an example of this form
Kita boleh memetik "Philosophie de la Misère" Proudhon sebagai contoh bentuk ini

The Socialistic Bourgeoisie want all the advantages of modern social conditions
Borjuasi Sosialistik mahukan semua kelebihan keadaan sosial moden

but the Socialistic Bourgeoisie don't necessarily want the resulting struggles and dangers

tetapi Borjuasi Sosialistik tidak semestinya mahukan perjuangan dan bahaya yang terhasil

They desire the existing state of society, minus its revolutionary and disintegrating elements

Mereka menginginkan keadaan masyarakat yang sedia ada, tolak unsur-unsur revolusioner dan hancurnya

in other words, they wish for a Bourgeoisie without a proletariat

dalam erti kata lain, mereka menginginkan Borjuasi tanpa proletariat

The Bourgeoisie naturally conceives the world in which it is supreme to be the best

Borjuasi secara semula jadi membayangkan dunia di mana ia adalah tertinggi untuk menjadi yang terbaik

and Bourgeoisie Socialism develops this comfortable conception into various more or less complete systems

dan Sosialisme Borjuasi mengembangkan konsep yang selesa ini ke dalam pelbagai sistem yang lebih kurang lengkap

they would very much like the proletariat to march straightway into the social New Jerusalem

mereka sangat mahu proletariat berarak terus ke Baitulmaqdis Baru yang sosial

but in reality it requires the proletariat to remain within the bounds of existing society

tetapi pada hakikatnya ia memerlukan proletariat untuk kekal dalam batas-batas masyarakat sedia ada

they ask the proletariat to cast away all their hateful ideas concerning the Bourgeoisie

mereka meminta proletariat untuk membuang semua idea kebencian mereka mengenai Borjuasi

there is a second more practical, but less systematic, form of this Socialism

terdapat bentuk kedua yang lebih praktikal, tetapi kurang sistematik, Sosialisme ini

this form of socialism sought to depreciate every revolutionary movement in the eyes of the working class

Bentuk sosialisme ini berusaha untuk merendahkan setiap gerakan revolusioner di mata kelas pekerja

they argue no mere political reform could be of any advantage to them

mereka berpendapat tiada pembaharuan politik semata-mata boleh memberi kelebihan kepada mereka

only a change in the material conditions of existence in economic relations are of benefit

hanya perubahan dalam keadaan material kewujudan dalam hubungan ekonomi yang bermanfaat

like communism, this form of socialism advocates for a change in the material conditions of existence

Seperti komunisme, bentuk sosialisme ini menyokong perubahan dalam keadaan material kewujudan

however, this form of socialism by no means suggests the abolition of the Bourgeoisie relations of production

walau bagaimanapun, bentuk sosialisme ini sama sekali tidak mencadangkan pemansuhan hubungan pengeluaran Borjuasi

the abolition of the Bourgeoisie relations of production can only be achieved through a revolution

pemansuhan hubungan pengeluaran Borjuasi hanya boleh dicapai melalui revolusi

but instead of a revolution, this form of socialism suggests administrative reforms

Tetapi bukannya revolusi, bentuk sosialisme ini mencadangkan pembaharuan pentadbiran

and these administrative reforms would be based on the continued existence of these relations

dan pembaharuan pentadbiran ini akan berdasarkan kewujudan berterusan hubungan ini

reforms, therefore, that in no respect affect the relations between capital and labour

pembaharuan, oleh itu, yang tidak menjejaskan hubungan antara modal dan buruh

at best, such reforms lessen the cost and simplify the
administrative work of Bourgeoisie government

paling baik, pembaharuan sedemikian mengurangkan kos dan
memudahkan kerja pentadbiran kerajaan Borjuasi

Bourgeois Socialism attains adequate expression, when, and
only when, it becomes a mere figure of speech

Sosialisme Borjuis mencapai ekspresi yang mencukupi,
apabila, dan hanya apabila, ia menjadi kiasan semata-mata

Free trade: for the benefit of the working class

Perdagangan bebas: untuk kepentingan kelas pekerja

Protective duties: for the benefit of the working class

Tugas perlindungan: untuk kepentingan kelas pekerja

Prison Reform: for the benefit of the working class

Pembaharuan Penjara: untuk kepentingan kelas pekerja

This is the last word and the only seriously meant word of
Bourgeoisie Socialism

Ini adalah perkataan terakhir dan satu-satunya perkataan
Sosialisme Borjuasi yang dimaksudkan secara serius

It is summed up in the phrase: the Bourgeoisie is a
Bourgeoisie for the benefit of the working class

Ia disimpulkan dalam frasa: Borjuasi adalah Borjuasi untuk
kepentingan kelas pekerja

3) Critical-Utopian Socialism and Communism
3) Sosialisme dan Komunisme Kritikal-Utopia

We do not here refer to that literature which has always given voice to the demands of the proletariat
Di sini kita tidak merujuk kepada kesusasteraan yang sentiasa menyuarakan tuntutan proletariat
this has been present in every great modern revolution, such as the writings of Babeuf and others
ini telah hadir dalam setiap revolusi moden yang hebat, seperti tulisan Babeuf dan lain-lain
The first direct attempts of the proletariat to attain its own ends necessarily failed
Percubaan langsung pertama proletariat untuk mencapai tujuannya sendiri semestinya gagal
these attempts were made in times of universal excitement, when feudal society was being overthrown
Percubaan ini dibuat pada masa keseronokan sejagat, apabila masyarakat feudal digulingkan
the then undeveloped state of the proletariat led to those attempts failing
keadaan proletariat yang belum berkembang ketika itu membawa kepada percubaan itu gagal
and they failed due to the absence of the economic conditions for its emancipation
dan mereka gagal kerana ketiadaan keadaan ekonomi untuk pembebasannya
conditions that had yet to be produced, and could be produced by the impending Bourgeoisie epoch alone
keadaan yang masih belum dihasilkan, dan boleh dihasilkan oleh zaman Borjuasi yang akan datang sahaja
The revolutionary literature that accompanied these first movements of the proletariat had necessarily a reactionary character

Kesusasteraan revolusioner yang mengiringi pergerakan pertama proletariat ini semestinya mempunyai watak reaksioner

This literature inculcated universal asceticism and social levelling in its crudest form

Kesusasteraan ini menanamkan pertapaan sejagat dan meratakan sosial dalam bentuknya yang paling kasar

The Socialist and Communist systems, properly so called, spring into existence in the early undeveloped period

Sistem Sosialis dan Komunis, yang dipanggil, wujud pada zaman awal yang belum dibangunkan

Saint-Simon, Fourier, Owen and others, described the struggle between proletariat and Bourgeoisie (see Section 1)

Saint-Simon, Fourier, Owen dan lain-lain, menggambarkan perjuangan antara proletariat dan Borjuasi (lihat Bahagian 1)

The founders of these systems see, indeed, the class antagonisms

Pengasas sistem ini melihat, sememangnya, antagonisme kelas

they also see the action of the decomposing elements, in the prevailing form of society

mereka juga melihat tindakan unsur-unsur yang mereput, dalam bentuk masyarakat yang lazim

But the proletariat, as yet in its infancy, offers to them the spectacle of a class without any historical initiative

Tetapi proletariat, yang masih di peringkat awal, menawarkan kepada mereka tontonan kelas tanpa sebarang inisiatif sejarah

they see the spectacle of a social class without any independent political movement

mereka melihat tontonan kelas sosial tanpa sebarang gerakan politik bebas

the development of class antagonism keeps even pace with the development of industry

Perkembangan antagonisme kelas seiring dengan perkembangan industri

so the economic situation does not as yet offer to them the material conditions for the emancipation of the proletariat

Oleh itu, keadaan ekonomi belum lagi menawarkan kepada mereka syarat-syarat material untuk pembebasan proletariat
They therefore search after a new social science, after new social laws, that are to create these conditions
Oleh itu, mereka mencari sains sosial baru, selepas undang-undang sosial baru, yang akan mewujudkan syarat-syarat ini
historical action is to yield to their personal inventive action
tindakan sejarah adalah untuk tunduk kepada tindakan inventif peribadi mereka
historically created conditions of emancipation are to yield to fantastic conditions
Keadaan pembebasan yang dicipta secara sejarah adalah untuk tunduk kepada keadaan yang hebat
and the gradual, spontaneous class-organisation of the proletariat is to yield to the organisation of society
dan organisasi kelas proletariat yang beransur-ansur dan spontan adalah untuk tunduk kepada organisasi masyarakat
the organisation of society specially contrived by these inventors
organisasi masyarakat yang direka khas oleh pencipta-pencipta ini
Future history resolves itself, in their eyes, into the propaganda and the practical carrying out of their social plans
Sejarah masa depan menyelesaikan dirinya sendiri, di mata mereka, ke dalam propaganda dan pelaksanaan praktikal rancangan sosial mereka
In the formation of their plans they are conscious of caring chiefly for the interests of the working class
Dalam pembentukan rancangan mereka, mereka sedar untuk menjaga kepentingan kelas pekerja
Only from the point of view of being the most suffering class does the proletariat exist for them
Hanya dari sudut pandangan sebagai kelas yang paling menderita, proletariat wujud untuk mereka

The undeveloped state of the class struggle and their own surroundings inform their opinions

Keadaan perjuangan kelas yang belum berkembang dan persekitaran mereka sendiri memaklumkan pendapat mereka

Socialists of this kind consider themselves far superior to all class antagonisms

Sosialis seperti ini menganggap diri mereka jauh lebih unggul daripada semua antagonisme kelas

They want to improve the condition of every member of society, even that of the most favoured

Mereka mahu memperbaiki keadaan setiap ahli masyarakat, walaupun yang paling digemari

Hence, they habitually appeal to society at large, without distinction of class

Oleh itu, mereka biasanya merayu kepada masyarakat secara amnya, tanpa membezakan kelas

nay, they appeal to society at large by preference to the ruling class

tidak, mereka merayu kepada masyarakat secara amnya dengan keutamaan kepada kelas pemerintah

to them, all it requires is for others to understand their system

Bagi mereka, apa yang diperlukan ialah orang lain memahami sistem mereka

because how can people fail to see that the best possible plan is for the best possible state of society?

Kerana bagaimana orang boleh gagal melihat bahawa rancangan terbaik adalah untuk keadaan masyarakat yang terbaik?

Hence, they reject all political, and especially all revolutionary, action

Oleh itu, mereka menolak semua tindakan politik, dan terutamanya semua revolusioner

they wish to attain their ends by peaceful means

mereka ingin mencapai tujuan mereka dengan cara yang aman

they endeavour, by small experiments, which are necessarily doomed to failure

mereka berusaha, dengan eksperimen kecil, yang semestinya ditakdirkan untuk gagal

and by the force of example they try to pave the way for the new social Gospel

dan dengan kekuatan teladan mereka cuba membuka jalan bagi Injil sosial yang baru

Such fantastic pictures of future society, painted at a time when the proletariat is still in a very undeveloped state

Gambar-gambar hebat masyarakat masa depan, dilukis pada masa proletariat masih dalam keadaan yang sangat belum maju

and it still has but a fantastical conception of its own position

dan ia masih mempunyai konsep fantastik tentang kedudukannya sendiri

but their first instinctive yearnings correspond with the yearnings of the proletariat

tetapi kerinduan naluri pertama mereka sepadan dengan kerinduan proletariat

both yearn for a general reconstruction of society

Kedua-duanya mendambakan pembinaan semula masyarakat secara umum

But these Socialist and Communist publications also contain a critical element

Tetapi penerbitan Sosialis dan Komunis ini juga mengandungi unsur kritikal

They attack every principle of existing society

Mereka menyerang setiap prinsip masyarakat sedia ada

Hence they are full of the most valuable materials for the enlightenment of the working class

Oleh itu mereka penuh dengan bahan yang paling berharga untuk pencerahan kelas pekerja

they propose abolition of the distinction between town and country, and the family

mereka mencadangkan pemansuhan perbezaan antara bandar dan desa, dan keluarga

the abolition of the carrying on of industries for the account of private individuals

pemansuhan menjalankan industri untuk akaun individu persendirian

and the abolition of the wage system and the proclamation of social harmony

dan pemansuhan sistem upah dan pengisytiharan keharmonian sosial

the conversion of the functions of the State into a mere superintendence of production

penukaran fungsi Negara kepada pengawasan pengeluaran semata-mata

all these proposals, point solely to the disappearance of class antagonisms

Semua cadangan ini, menunjuk semata-mata kepada hilangnya antagonisme kelas

class antagonisms were, at that time, only just cropping up

Antagonisme kelas, pada masa itu, baru sahaja muncul

in these publications these class antagonisms are recognised in their earliest, indistinct and undefined forms only

Dalam penerbitan ini, antagonisme kelas ini diiktiraf dalam bentuk yang paling awal, tidak jelas dan tidak ditentukan sahaja

These proposals, therefore, are of a purely Utopian character

Oleh itu, cadangan ini adalah watak Utopia semata-mata

The significance of Critical-Utopian Socialism and Communism bears an inverse relation to historical development

Kepentingan Sosialisme Kritikal-Utopia dan Komunisme mempunyai hubungan songsang dengan perkembangan sejarah

the modern class struggle will develop and continue to take definite shape

Perjuangan kelas moden akan berkembang dan terus mengambil bentuk yang pasti

this fantastic standing from the contest will lose all practical value

Kedudukan hebat daripada pertandingan ini akan kehilangan semua nilai praktikal

these fantastic attacks on class antagonisms will lose all theoretical justification

Serangan hebat terhadap antagonisme kelas ini akan kehilangan semua justifikasi teori

the originators of these systems were, in many respects, revolutionary

Pencetus sistem ini, dalam banyak aspek, revolusioner

but their disciples have, in every case, formed mere reactionary sects

tetapi murid-murid mereka, dalam setiap kes, membentuk mazhab reaksioner semata-mata

They hold tightly to the original views of their masters

Mereka berpegang teguh pada pandangan asal tuan mereka

but these views are in opposition to the progressive historical development of the proletariat

Tetapi pandangan ini bertentangan dengan perkembangan sejarah progresif proletariat

They, therefore, endeavour, and that consistently, to deaden the class struggle

Oleh itu, mereka berusaha, dan secara konsisten, untuk mematikan perjuangan kelas

and they consistently endeavour to reconcile the class antagonisms

dan mereka secara konsisten berusaha untuk mendamaikan antagonisme kelas

They still dream of experimental realisation of their social Utopias

Mereka masih mengimpikan realisasi eksperimen Utopia sosial mereka

they still dream of founding isolated "phalansteres" and establishing "Home Colonies"

mereka masih bermimpi untuk mengasaskan "phalansteres" terpencil dan menubuhkan "Tanah Jajahan Rumah"

they dream of setting up a "Little Icaria"—duodecimo editions of the New Jerusalem

mereka bermimpi untuk menubuhkan "Little Icaria"—edisi duodecimo Baitulmaqdis Baru

and they dream to realise all these castles in the air

dan mereka bermimpi untuk merealisasikan semua istana ini di udara

they are compelled to appeal to the feelings and purses of the bourgeois

mereka terpaksa merayu kepada perasaan dan dompet borjuis

By degrees they sink into the category of the reactionary conservative Socialists depicted above

Secara bertahap mereka tenggelam ke dalam kategori Sosialis konservatif reaksioner yang digambarkan di atas

they differ from these only by more systematic pedantry

Mereka berbeza daripada ini hanya dengan pedantri yang lebih sistematik

and they differ by their fanatical and superstitious belief in the miraculous effects of their social science

dan mereka berbeza dengan kepercayaan fanatik dan khurafat mereka terhadap kesan ajaib sains sosial mereka

They, therefore, violently oppose all political action on the part of the working class

Oleh itu, mereka menentang keras semua tindakan politik di pihak kelas pekerja

such action, according to them, can only result from blind unbelief in the new Gospel

tindakan sedemikian, menurut mereka, hanya boleh terhasil daripada ketidakpercayaan buta kepada Injil baru

The Owenites in England, and the Fourierists in France, respectively, oppose the Chartists and the "Réformistes"

Orang Owenit di England, dan Fourierist di Perancis, masing-masing, menentang Chartists dan "Réformistes"

Position of the Communists in Relation to the Various Existing Opposision Parties
Kedudukan Komunis berhubung dengan pelbagai parti pembangkang sedia ada

Section II has made clear the relations of the Communists to the existing working-class parties
Bahagian II telah menjelaskan hubungan Komunis dengan parti-parti kelas pekerja sedia ada
such as the Chartists in England, and the Agrarian Reformers in America
seperti Chartists di England, dan Reformis Agraria di Amerika
The Communists fight for the attainment of the immediate aims
Komunis berjuang untuk mencapai matlamat segera
they fight for the enforcement of the momentary interests of the working class
mereka berjuang untuk penguatkuasaan kepentingan seketika kelas pekerja
but in the political movement of the present, they also represent and take care of the future of that movement
Tetapi dalam pergerakan politik masa kini, mereka juga mewakili dan menjaga masa depan pergerakan itu
In France the Communists ally themselves with the Social-Democrats
Di Perancis Komunis bersekutu dengan Sosial-Demokrat
and they position themselves against the conservative and radical Bourgeoisie
dan mereka meletakkan diri mereka menentang Borjuasi konservatif dan radikal

however, they reserve the right to take up a critical position
in regard to phrases and illusions traditionally handed down
from the great Revolution

walau bagaimanapun, mereka berhak untuk mengambil
kedudukan kritikal berkenaan dengan frasa dan ilusi yang
secara tradisinya diturunkan daripada Revolusi besar

**In Switzerland they support the Radicals, without losing
sight of the fact that this party consists of antagonistic
elements**

Di Switzerland mereka menyokong Radikal, tanpa melupakan
hakikat bahawa parti ini terdiri daripada unsur-unsur
antagonis

**partly of Democratic Socialists, in the French sense, partly of
radical Bourgeoisie**

sebahagiannya daripada Sosialis Demokratik, dalam erti kata
Perancis, sebahagiannya daripada Borjuasi radikal

**In Poland they support the party that insists on an agrarian
revolution as the prime condition for national emancipation**

Di Poland mereka menyokong parti yang menegaskan
revolusi agraria sebagai syarat utama untuk pembebasan
negara

**that party which fomented the insurrection of Cracow in
1846**

parti yang mencetuskan pemberontakan Cracow pada tahun
1846

**In Germany they fight with the Bourgeoisie whenever it acts
in a revolutionary way**

Di Jerman mereka berjuang dengan Borjuasi apabila ia
bertindak dengan cara yang revolusioner

**against the absolute monarchy, the feudal squirearchy, and
the petty Bourgeoisie**

menentang monarki mutlak, squirearchy feudal, dan Borjuasi
kecil

**But they never cease, for a single instant, to instil into the
working class one particular idea**

Tetapi mereka tidak pernah berhenti, untuk sekejap, untuk menanamkan ke dalam kelas pekerja satu idea tertentu

the clearest possible recognition of the hostile antagonism between Bourgeoisie and proletariat

pengiktirafan yang paling jelas tentang antagonisme bermusuhan antara Borjuasi dan proletariat

so that the German workers may straightaway use the weapons at their disposal

supaya pekerja Jerman boleh terus menggunakan senjata yang mereka boleh gunakan

the social and political conditions that the Bourgeoisie must necessarily introduce along with its supremacy

keadaan sosial dan politik yang semestinya diperkenalkan oleh Borjuasi bersama-sama dengan ketuanannya

the fall of the reactionary classes in Germany is inevitable

kejatuhan kelas reaksioner di Jerman tidak dapat dielakkan

and then the fight against the Bourgeoisie itself may immediately begin

dan kemudian perjuangan menentang Borjuasi itu sendiri boleh segera bermula

The Communists turn their attention chiefly to Germany, because that country is on the eve of a Bourgeoisie revolution

Komunis mengalihkan perhatian mereka terutamanya kepada Jerman, kerana negara itu berada di malam revolusi Borjuasi

a revolution that is bound to be carried out under more advanced conditions of European civilisation

revolusi yang pasti akan dijalankan di bawah keadaan tamadun Eropah yang lebih maju

and it is bound to be carried out with a much more developed proletariat

dan ia pasti akan dilaksanakan dengan proletariat yang jauh lebih maju

a proletariat more advanced than that of England was in the seventeenth, and of France in the eighteenth century

proletariat yang lebih maju daripada England pada abad ketujuh belas, dan Perancis pada abad kelapan belas

and because the Bourgeoisie revolution in Germany will be but the prelude to an immediately following proletarian revolution

dan kerana revolusi Borjuasi di Jerman akan menjadi permulaan kepada revolusi proletar sejurus selepas itu

In short, the Communists everywhere support every revolutionary movement against the existing social and political order of things

Pendek kata, Komunis di mana-mana menyokong setiap gerakan revolusioner menentang susunan sosial dan politik yang sedia ada

In all these movements they bring to the front, as the leading question in each, the property question

Dalam semua pergerakan ini mereka membawa ke hadapan, sebagai persoalan utama dalam setiap persoalan, persoalan harta

no matter what its degree of development is in that country at the time

Tidak kira apa tahap pembangunannya di negara itu pada masa itu

Finally, they labour everywhere for the union and agreement of the democratic parties of all countries

Akhirnya, mereka bekerja di mana-mana untuk kesatuan dan persetujuan parti demokrasi semua negara

The Communists disdain to conceal their views and aims

Komunis menghina untuk menyembunyikan pandangan dan matlamat mereka

They openly declare that their ends can be attained only by the forcible overthrow of all existing social conditions

Mereka secara terbuka mengisytiharkan bahawa tujuan mereka boleh dicapai hanya dengan penggulingan paksa semua keadaan sosial yang ada

Let the ruling classes tremble at a Communistic revolution

Biarkan kelas pemerintah gemetar pada revolusi Komunis

The proletarians have nothing to lose but their chains
Proletar tidak mempunyai apa-apa untuk hilang selain rantai mereka
They have a world to win
Mereka mempunyai dunia untuk menang
WORKING MEN OF ALL COUNTRIES, UNITE!
LELAKI PEKERJA DARI SEMUA NEGARA, BERSATU!

www.ingramcontent.com/pod-product-compliance
Lightning Source LLC
Chambersburg PA
CBHW011738020426
42333CB00024B/2949